People of Florence

People of Florence

A STUDY IN LOCALITY 

JOSEPH MACLEOD

> Peoples will not die;
> The tail curls stronger when you lop the head.
> They writhe at every wound, and multiply.
> *Elizabeth Barrett Browning*

South Brunswick
New York: A. S. Barnes and Company

One of the most interesting and often revealing aspects of other people is why they are where they are. In some cases it is where the work is; in others it can be from sentimental attachment, circles of friends, reluctance to move, or hope, or despair.

In this book I have tried to indicate or to imply, without writing autobiographically, how a casual visitor to Florence can become a resident imperceptibly and almost unawares. I hoped not to romanticise a city too easily raptured about. Perhaps I have not given enough of the picturesque or immediately attractive.

The main chapters are interleaved with short sketches which usually have a bearing on what has gone before. The last three main chapters are somewhat polemical. They grew so from the facts, not from any theory. But a writer on a subject near to his heart can be forgiven for sounding an alarum.

Naturally I hope this considered account of the people of Florence will encourage readers to go and meet them, indeed to live among them, who might not otherwise do so. But my purpose has been not propaganda but an accurate impression of the actual people.

I have put at the end a list of books from which i have drawn special information or ideas. In this kind of book a scholarly *apparatus criticus* would be out of place, even in the compiled chapter on theatre history.

A small part of the text has been published in articles for *The Times* and *The Spectator*. I am grateful for permission to incorporate this.

Florence, august 1967

CONTENTS

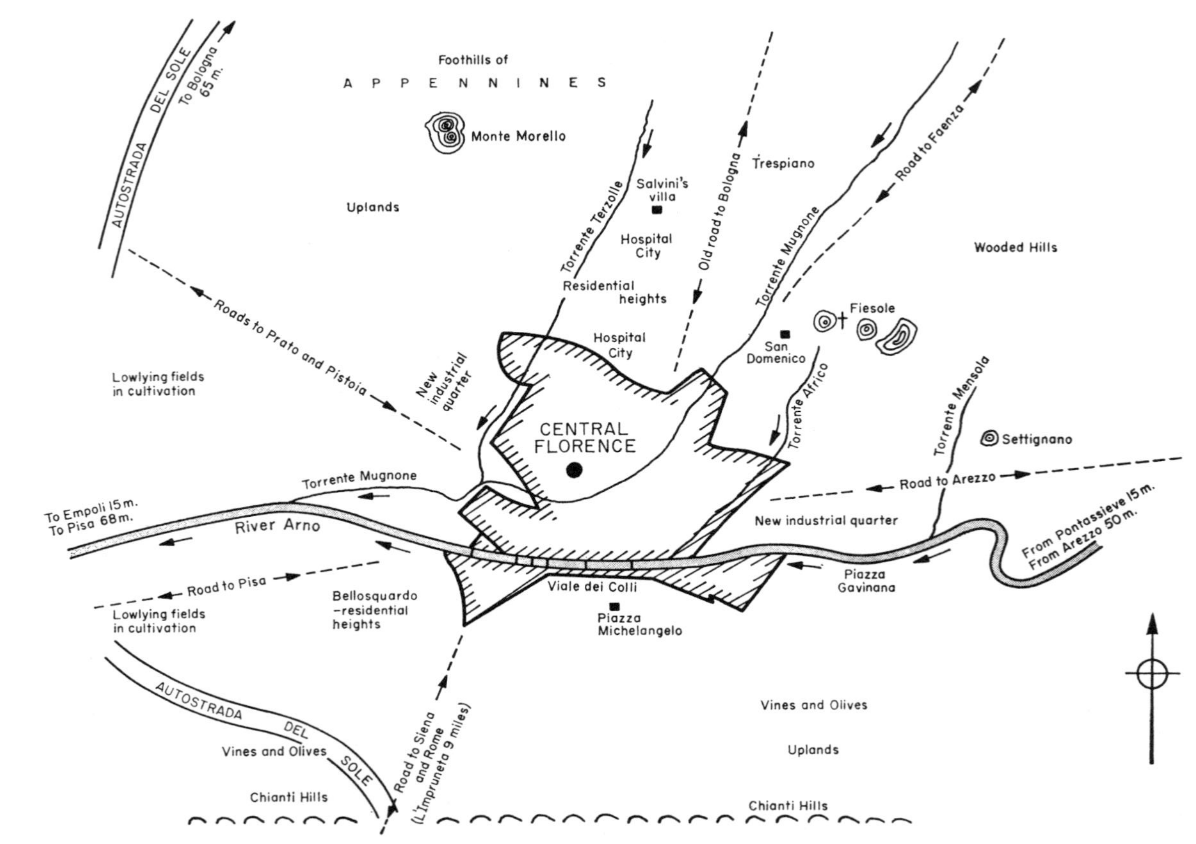

Foothills of
APPENNINES
Monte Morello
Salvini's villa
Trespiano
Uplands
Hospital City
Old road to Bologna
Road to Faenza
Residential heights
Torrente Terzolle
Torrente Mugnone
Wooded Hills
Hospital City
Fiesole
Roads to Prato and Pistoia
San Domenico
New industrial quarter
CENTRAL FLORENCE
Torrente Affrico
Settignano
Torrente Mensola
Lowlying fields in cultivation
To Empoli 15 m.
To Pisa 68m.
River Arno
Road to Arezzo
New industrial quarter
From Pontassieve 15 m.
From Arezzo 50 m.
Torrente Mugnone
Road to Pisa
Bellosguardo -residential heights
Viale dei Colli
Piazza Gavinana
AUTOSTRADA DEL SOLE
To Bologna 65 m.
Lowlying fields in cultivation
Road to Siena and Rome (L'Impruneta 9 miles)
Piazza Michelangelo
Vines and Olives
Uplands
Chianti Hills
AUTOSTRADA DEL SOLE
Vines and Olives
Chianti Hills

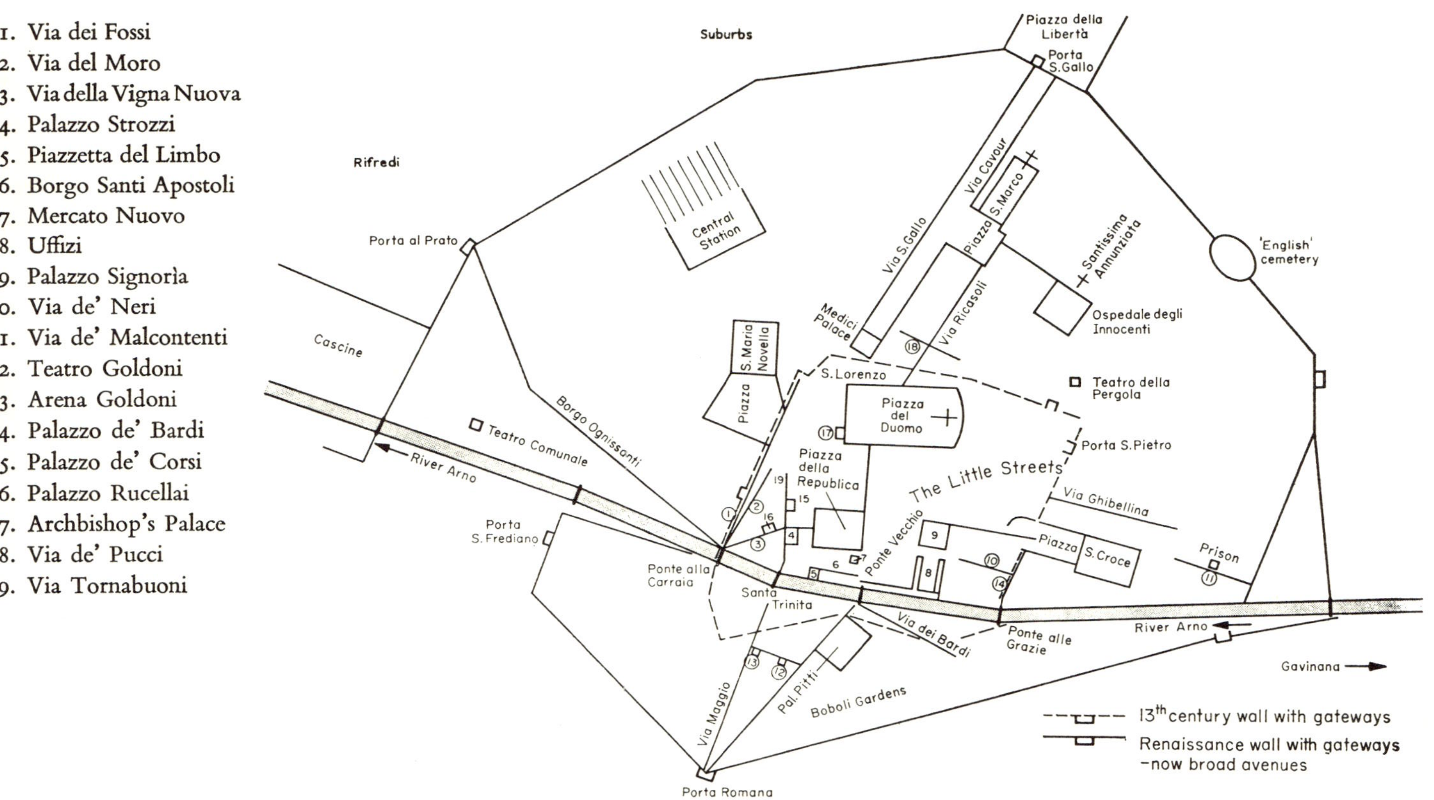

1. Via dei Fossi
2. Via del Moro
3. Via della Vigna Nuova
4. Palazzo Strozzi
5. Piazzetta del Limbo
6. Borgo Santi Apostoli
7. Mercato Nuovo
8. Uffizi
9. Palazzo Signorìa
10. Via de' Neri
11. Via de' Malcontenti
12. Teatro Goldoni
13. Arena Goldoni
14. Palazzo de' Bardi
15. Palazzo de' Corsi
16. Palazzo Rucellai
17. Archbishop's Palace
18. Via de' Pucci
19. Via Tornabuoni

I

Illustrious but Dead

This begins with the dead because the whole was to be a new life.

'Where do we go?' I asked, as she settled her new self into the maroon Alvis. I would have driven to the moon in such company.

'Florence' she said. So we left Rome, as hundreds of young men in wigs on the Grand Tour had arrived there, by the Porta del Popolo.

Rome is what Italians call a *civetta*, the little owl *athene noctua*, which they say calls '*Tutto mio! Tutto mio!*' Which is to say that Rome is a flirt, who wants everybody and in her own way. She usually gets them.

On earlier visits, however, I had found her grandiose, illustrious, but dead. She receives, I thought, into the recesses of her ruins, but never gives out of them. Then, overnight, she played with me. 'Dead? Grandiose?' whispered the Temple of Vesta. The Forums laid-on a daffodil knocking at a fallen pillar, and a sunset which splashed the top tiered arches of the Colosseum blood-red as I entered the no longer blood-stained arena of the gladiators.

Cities can talk as animals and trees talk; and in much the same way. Out of her immensity Rome spoke to me with small voices for almost a year after that, whether I was in her or away from her. Especially when in her, in the crooked pavementless lanes west of the Piazza di Spagna near the Via della Scrofa: to me, munching piquant *pasta alla*

Matriciana[1] alone in trattorías: to a visitor, tied and waiting to live.

The tie and the waiting ended with this drive to Florence, through glens as soft as Perthshire. Florence, on my way south, I had deliberately avoided: a place where Dante met Beatrice by a victorian Arno (picture postcard of my youth), interesting only to learned connoisseurs of art, and filled with prototypes of bank buildings. In any case I was then coming not to Italy but to Rome.

'A month at the most, perhaps.' And we set about calling on Florence.

Florence was in a mess. The tram lines were being pulled up. It was impossible for the Alvis, if she drove into the Piazza del Duomo, to drive out of it again without being sent round temporarily one-way streets to the point she had come in at. And all motorised visitors find themselves sooner or later at the Duomo, since you can hardly cross the city without passing it.

Also it was raining. It rained all december. It often does.

Ignorant visitors should never tour Florence by guide-book, but leave the book in the hotel bedroom and wander in and out of doorways. When they come across the carved Annunciation in Santa Croce[2] or a picture of a saint in Ognissanti, let them stop and look, for they won't ignore them, and put the names of Donatello or Botticelli to them later, when resting their feet.

I wandered into the 'English' Cemetery, not knowing why. Cemeteries smell of autumn damp. This one was very autumnal and distinctly damp, an island knoll in a lake of roaring and swishing traffic. Such measures as the italian government

---

[1] Choose your spaghetti or other *pasta* for its sugo or sauce. Tomato paste, cheese, meat, are not the only italian *sughi*. Try them *alle Vongole* (clams, with parsley and a little garlic), or *alla Carbonara* (fried with chopped bacon, sausage and a raw egg) or *alla Matriciana* which contains chopped bacon and chillis. There are many others.

[2] Santa Croce: temporary national Pantheon-to-be, once; full of exquisite frescoes and hideous monuments. Ognissanti (All Saints): partly covered with Baroque, easy of access to rich Americans in two of the most luxurious hotels.

has taken to reduce traffic noise by silencers and other devices had not yet been taken: the din of Florence's narrow streets was unendurable. But most Italians love noise. More is paid for the roar of a car than for its horse power; and the lowest gears are used to produce the highest quantity of phons and decibels.

Italian children are born with operatic lungs and shout before they speak. When they grow up, even if gentle and well bred, they talk in loud clear voices simultaneously to each other, or even to nobody like rival barkers at a fair.

On the island even in the middle of that wide avenue the din of traffic was inescapable. It somehow made splashes of raindrops from cypresses more audible, not less.

There is no guide nor plan to the graveyard. I heaved on an old iron bell-pull, beneath which there is now an electric buzzer, and was admitted to solitude. I walked up one of the two small lanes between waist-high box hedges, and soon came upon The Grave.

Its greying white casket stood before three cypresses among young cherry trees, an entablature of wet blobby semibreves. The lassitude of the coarse grass was lank. I did not know that in spring it would be full of wild tuscan anemones.

The rod-surround was rusty.

Lord Leighton's smudged casket proved unexpectedly pleasant, with inlaid black classical figures which suggested De Chirico's set for *Le Bal.*[1] Some were greek lyres supported by olive branches. On the grave below, a real olive branch had been laid, shaped as a wreath.

There was also a bunch of plastic lily-of-the-valley.

One of the cypresses creaked in the dreich wind. The cry seemed to come from an unquiet tomb.

I was not a great admirer of Elizabeth Barrett Browning's

[1] Giorgio de Chirico was much sought after for the strange atmosphere of his pictured piazzas with marble horses and statues and pillars. He designed in this classical-architectural style the sets and costumes for the Diaghilev ballet *Le Bal.* Nowadays his horsemen ride twistedly through enchanted forests.

poetry, but I was fond of the Brownings and loved *The Ring and the Book* when I was young. That was long ago.

Someone told Ezra Pound that the mantle of Browning had fallen on him: and Pound wrote to me that it had fallen from him on me. But that too was long ago, and Pound was always kind to young poets.

Next to E.B.B. lies Fanny, wife of Holman Hunt. She died in Florence in december 1866 'in the first year of her marriage.' That year Holman Hunt painted *Isabella and the Pot of Basil*, one of the saddest of Preraphaelite pictures, the theme from Boccaccio or Keats; for Keats drew much of his narrative poem from the story in the *Decameron*, though he placed it in Florence not Messina, and altered the heroine's name to Isabella from Lisabetta, as it is in my edition anyway. However she was called, this girl's lover was murdered by her brothers; and she dug up his grave and reburied his head in a pot of basil, which she wept over till she too died. I was sad for Holman Hunt and his pretty young wife.

But it was not these graves which interested me, nor that of A. H. Clough[1] nearby. I passed on. Many solid-looking superstructures of graves were smashed like chocolate easter eggs. The more recent inscriptions, cut too lightly, had all but vanished.

At last I came on a slab of more white and greying marble, and was standing higher than the bones of my turbulent hero. Landor's famous quatrain[2] is patently untrue in its first line; he strove with nearly all—though very likely few of the bureaucrats were worth his strife. This makes one wonder if the last line is any truer. Was that old lion, who threw his cook out of the window and was gentle with children, really ever

---

[1] I am glad to know that in Rugby School Chapel Rupert Brooke, long exiled to a distant pillar because his poetry was not quite nice, has now been admitted to Poets' Corner with the other Rugby poets A. H. Clough and Matthew Arnold.

[2] *I strove with none, for none was worth my strife.*
    Nature I loved, and next to nature, Art.
  I warmed both hands before the fire of life.
    It sinks; and I am ready to depart.

16

ready to depart? How many such lovers of life are? Would I be? For to stand by a grave is to have one foot already in it. For everybody at all graves.

It is a pity that Swinburne, who wrote a panegyric on him in the *Encyclopaedia Britannica*, should have been the one to compose his epitaph. Alliteration and admiration together made him fall into bathos.

> '. . . *So shall thy lovers, come from far,*
>   '*Mix with thy name*' (Florence's)
> '*As morning star with evening star*
>   '*His faultless fame.*'

But who now reads the vivid historical dialogues of that Browning of english prose? who now remembers the verse which this fourth Rugby poet wrote in seventy years of unceasing energy? who cares about victorian residents, dead in Florence, Italy?

The rain went on falling. I too had had enough.

I passed more graves: french, italian, german, russian, irish; few american, because the cemetery was closed before Florence grew really popular in the United States.

But many Scots, each proudly asserting scottish domicile to the end—and after. Ancrum of Roxburgh, Mackenzie of Hartfield, Ross-shire, Isabella Scott of Gala N.B., and Thomas Tod of Edinburgh who had been attaché at the Court of Tuscany.

A crowd of dead co-nationals in a foreign burial-ground makes one die personally in many pieces. So I left the illustrious dead on their modest mound.

Illustrious but dead! Was Florence to prove the same?

2

'O Sole Splendido!'

In the first week of january each year in Fiesole it is possible to sit on the low kerb outside the house and eat lunch in shirt sleeves. From a passing farm cart drawn by two white oxen (or often white milk-cows) a voice may call *'Buon appetito!'* It may be the first and the last time a visitor hears that fading courtesy among strangers, though it continues among fellow-diners and friends.

There is a road that had been called the Street of the Cart, very suitably because it is just wide enough for a cart to pass through walls of almost etruscan masonry, which are even built in places on actual etruscan walls. For the Etruscans built Fiesole years before the Romans built their Florentia. But now this is called 'Giuseppe Verdi Street,' like hundreds of others in the cities of Italy, where each Toponomastic Department copies another.

A thousand feet below lies all Florence. The Arno wriggles into the western hills, each fold a different colour at sunset, pink, pale blue, grey, orange, silver, like coloured lights seen through a torn curtain. At lunchtime it is all silver in this distant enchantment. As a rule, close up, it flows dun.

No tourists came to study the famous view. They did not know of the january sun. I was more visitor than tourist. An ignorant one. Not knowing the ornithology of Italy, I mistook for some yellow continental finches a pair of canaries, escaped from an old lady nearby. It was warm and sunny as we ate our *panini* of raw ham in rough unsalted tuscan bread, and drank our sophisticated wine.

18

'Sophisticated' wine in italian does not mean smart wine nor refined wine; it means a mixture of local third-class grapes brought up to the alcoholic-content-grade the Italians insist on, with wine of more strength than flavour sent from the South in demijohns.

We did not mind. In the warm sun we were comfortable, but poor, but very happy. A radio set kept playing from a cottage a popular song called *O Quest'Amore Splendido*.

Within a day or two the snow came. In Fiesole there was no garage then: and even in Britain it was still nominally illegal to leave a car in the street all night. When I was advised to stand the Alvis out in a somewhat broader street than that of The Cart, I said snow was bad for the paint. Smiling friendly faces reassured the foreign visitor. 'It never snows in Fiesole, Mister.' I did not yet know enough not to believe this, but suspected the Highland 'Only a mile and a bittock' which falsely encourages a traveller onward to his last ten exhausted miles out of sheer goodwill and pity.

Not only snow came, but blizzards and ice. In neither of our rooms was any heating. If we were lucky, a landlady would bring us a *scaldino*, a small basket of earthenware filled with charcoal. Every now and then we blew on this, because the ash blankets the heat. Every now and then we transferred it from hands to feet and feet to hands, and even to noses, as the blood began to congeal in our extremities. I thought of my boyhood heroes Robert Falcon Scott and 'Titus' Oates, and wished I could return, in my light winter clothes, to Scotland.

We had found work as translators, and typed by shifts, each tapping till hands stiffened and *scaldino* could take typewriter's place. The best way to keep the feet from freezing during work was to put them in bed.

At night, again if we were lucky, our landladies put priests in our beds. Priests in oldfashioned italian beds are subjects of as much misunderstanding and as many broad jokes as pigs in oldfashioned scottish ones.[1] They are a sort of open-sided upturned sussex trug, from the lath roof of which the *scaldino* is hung until bedtime, and seldom sets the bed on fire. They are more fierce and friendly than a rubber hotwaterbottle. They do not make one feel buried alive in heat as an electric blanket does.

Every evening, having no kitchens, we put on further layers of clothes and footwool and went down to the *trattoría* for supper. I say 'went' because this wide verb includes crawling, stepping, sliding, crunching, pausing, balancing, groping and starting again. There is hardly a level street in Fiesole. Every evening we were the only living creatures out. Not a dog nor a cat nor a rat. We went with laughter.

The *trattoría* was kept by a lady from the Romagna, country of Maresa's family, where the eating is among the best in Italy. So it was here. We had arranged a meal a day throughout the winter at about 5s. 10d. each. For this we got *pasta* of various kinds, on sundays *lasagne al forno*.[2] The Signora Lena made this on saturday nights, hanging the green sheets on backs of unoccupied chairs, of which, though the place was small, there were at that season many. We got veal or beef or chicken fried or roast, fruit and cheeses of various kinds, and as much good wine as we wanted. We wanted much.

The Signora Lena was a big, open, full-voiced lady with a handsome peasant face crowned by blue hair, who loved cats and the young. Several students of Florence University lodged in Fiesole, and to eat ran up bills with her, some high, as high as L.100,000 over the years. She never pressed. She trusted them to pay her back when they could. If they couldn't, or didn't, she let it pass, having helped when help was needed.

[1] In Scotland a pig was a stoneware jar or bottle used for whisky and several other purposes. Before hotwaterbottles existed (and these too were at first of stoneware; their stoppers sang like kettles) they were filled with hot water and put in the bed either bare or wrapped in flannel.

[2] Folded sheets of *pasta* interleaved with a rich *sugo* and baked in the oven. The green comes from spinach mixed into the pasta. This has been a delight since Dante's day.

The *trattoría* then had a terrazza at the back, vine-ribbed-over in summer, cool and welcoming, even if it had no view. The quality of the food got known down in Florence, and alert families coming up for summer coolth began to avoid the dearer restaurants. The Signora Lena had to expand. She (and her husband and son and cousin and later daughter-in-law) opened a second room and then roofed-in the terrazza. For the summer clients stayed on through the winters. The locals, who had gone for cheap meals into the kitchen, continued to have *polenta* and sausages[1] and other traditional food there long after the expansion. We too wanted *polenta* in the kitchen, but were told it wasn't good enough for us.

This family is now doing fine, and has expanded again, with a modern kitchen and a grill. But the success story does not end there: for in the modern kitchen, which is in the principal eating-room, the Signora Lena not only cooks with her own unfussed hands but keeps an eye on her client-friends at dozens of tables. In short, here is the only restaurant I have frequented in any country which did not lose either quality or atmosphere when it grew big. It is now lined with pictures by young artists, some probably in lieu of payment, others just on show in the hope of a sale, as is done by many young artists who cannot afford one-man exhibitions.

But as yet we are in winter, and have still to face ice and snow, whipped by the cruel north wind into swirling ropes like waterspouts, capering over street and piazza, and taunting a solitary streetside palm-tree, which flaps and crackles in miserable memory of Africa. The thermometer is now down to — 15° centigrade (27° of frost fahrenheit) and we feel sorry for the palm as we pass from the warmth of the *trattoría* to that of our evening bar on the main piazza. Here in those days the *espresso* machine was of the oldfashioned kind (soon to be

[1] *Polenta* is a kind of porridge made from maize flour. It has similar effects to those of oatmeal porridge and buckwheat *kasha*, in that it is excellent in cold wet weather, makes you feel you have eaten more than you have done, and can give weak stomachs indigestion.

scattered and sold–off all over Britain as the latest model) which roared and hissed like a Glasgow tram but gave good welcome to ice-gloved hands.

The son of the proprietor of the evening bar was a tall and handsome youth with a passion for reading. He knew Dickens and Balzac and Tolstoy in translation and was learning german. He could be teased into trying to say *fünf und fünfzig*. One sunday night I asked him why Orion was blue, when only Vega was a blue star. He rang up the Observatory. I bet him only a janitor would answer, but on the contrary a director replied, courteous and pleased, explaining that the colour depended on angles of rays in the frosty air, and thanking us for the inquiry.

The cold worked in. For the only time in my life I had a chilblain, which felt like frostbite and may have been. We developed colds in the head. We had fevers. On top of cold and fever I had conjunctivitis and hourly awaited trouble in the sinus. The Signora Lena sent her son up the hill with full hot suppers of broth and chicken in linen-wrapped pannikins with forks and spoons and knives. The son came back later to clear away. No extra charge.

But the little window of my bedroom had an ermine frame of snow lining the inside.

We got over that. Not perhaps with laughter. With adventure. The Alvis, anti-freezed, got over it too. Snow did her no harm, but later, in the summer, wine did. I washed her down by a little stream, using a wine-flask I had forgotten first to flush out. The vinegar faded the rear panel under my eyes.

So spring came, and the sun again. The entire hillside burst into wistaria blossom, on walls, in hedges, even up cypress trees where it mixed with climbing roses. This spectacle has a repeat performance in full summer, less showy perhaps; and minor scenes are given again in autumn excerpts.

Spring, Fiesole, new life, the words mean the same thing. With spring in new life at Fiesole I was given a new name.

On St Joseph's Day, which is the big festival and holiday of march, Italians make sweet fritters called in Tuscany *frittelle*. The Signora Lena handed round a plate of these after supper. I said they must be made specially for me, this being my *onomastico*.

'Your nameday? Is your name Giuseppe? *Auguri, Signor Giuseppe!*' And next morning (I am not exaggerating) it was *Buon giorno, Signor Giuseppe!* from the grocer, greengrocer, butcher, morning coffee-bar and even, I think, in the little post office. I knew I belonged.

Names are the most precious things we have in our inner lives. Most people are pleased with extra pleasure when recognised by name. Many still get a thrill at seeing their private names mentioned in public print. In a world where cities like Dunedin, Adelaide, New York, Washington and (for all I know) Babylon or Eldorado are to be known by postal numbers, in a world where insurance companies know their clients' troubles by rows of ciphers, a family name and a first name are a continuous reassurance of identity.

No one person is like any other, nor ever has been among the millions of millions of persons since the anthropoid apes and probably since the emergence of the animal brain. Nevertheless just as pictures are mere re-arrangements of lines, colours and forms already in existence, so we are mere re-arrangements of bits of other people in word, act, build, feature, tendencies and character. No human being likes this thought. From the first in society we resist it: some do so all their lives. We try to discover who we are. A dominant part of us selects facets, and lets other sides sink back into their subconscious origins (which are almost entirely other people from the ice age on). The selected self we often exaggerate, forcing it on other people, even with uncalled for and unjustifiable violence; even with murder. Thereby we exacerbate, not assuage, our discontents and frustrations (which also are other people). So we hang our personalities on a name as symbol of an incomplete self identifiable by other people long before we have identified ourselves.

I doubt if we do ever identify ourselves more than in the very small parts we have selected. In this, a crank, an 'average person,' and a genius are in the same position. The difference between a crank and a genius is that between a revolt and a revolution: if he is historically successful a man cannot be called a crank.

But whoever we are, other people continue to modify or affect us, even our selected selves. And we in our turn, small summations as we are of our locality in time and space, we too go on in part affecting and re-arranging others; and will do so with many we will never know or meet in the historical sweep from eternity to eternity.

In this sense the individual grows so infinitesimal as hardly to exist.

In my own case the problem of identity had been acuter than in many people's. Millions had called me by the christian name without knowing me: they had set up images of me not true to me, but so true to them that some acknowledged 'my' influence on them. Contrariwise, if one selected facet of my self had been that of a poet, nobody had ever called me by the names under or over which I had published verse. So this new name was doubly welcome. It was a new initiation, a really personal salute, an invitation from interest and liking to join a world I was interested in and liked.

What sort of a world was it?

There were still few tourists then; and when there were, and Maresa had to go often back to Rome, I sat on under the lime trees of the piazza in the hot summer evenings, drinking and talking with students and others who called me by this name; and was content not to have to go down to a florentine hotel and sleep to wake to sightsee. Though I had no idea why I was where I was, I felt more at home there than if I had been given the Freedom of the City.

3

View from a Hill

The three hills of fresh Fiesole rise on the north of Florence. Two of them are studded with houses, old dark turretted villas, new suntrap homes, balconied terraces, gardens over gardens, where tall magnolias stand, oranges and lemons in great pots, cypresses galore, a palm and a pomegranate or two, or persimmons whose reddening luscious globes ripen on unleaved branches into the fogs of winter.

The third hill, Monte Céceri, slopes higher and wilder, thick and dark with cypress, pine, juniper and oak; at whose foot Boccaccio placed his *Decameron* during an outbreak of the Plague.[1]

But little of Fiesole itself, other than its lissom campanile is seen from outside: for it lies between and behind its twin hills as secluded as when Florence was still a swamp, innocent as when Florence stole up, time and again, to destroy it. Still more etruscan than tuscan, its walls and tombs pioneered the architecture of roman baths and the roman theatre. Nobody now carries their undigested peacock to those baths; but the theatre, a rare first-century one, still holds three thousand spectators for Shakespeare, ballet, or costume plays on a stage backing into a garden under the dry sky of summer nights.

Visitors come up to see the eleventh century cathedral (somewhat restored) and to buy straw goods at the market across

---

[1] 100 short stories, earthy, funny, pitiful, cruel, active, lively, enchanting; set in an arcadian courtly villa of evacuees. The passages which english translations leave in the italian can easily be followed by novices with a dictionary.

the piazza. Mass on sunday mornings has to fight with the jukebox at the café opposite. For life is not wanting in a Fiesole summer, and being italian it is noisy life.

But many come up for quiet. They toil up one or other of the nearer hills. They find it on a little landing of the Via Verdi, precisely where we ate our january lunches; or at the fourteenth century franciscan monastery that crowns the wester hill at the point where stood a mediaeval fortress to scare and annoy the Florentines. Franciscan monasteries always crown hills. In Tuscany they are like Armada bonfires, almost in distant sight of one another, almost communicable by heliograph from hilltop to hilltop. This one, visible all over Florence, glints gold in the sunset.

Few visitors trudge up Monte Céceri, but residents do, to walk and even to work in its woods, loud with brown nightingales all day long, and lithe with large green lizards, and even surprising with leaf-green spiders. They pass the point where Leonardo da Vinci, looking out over Florence, is said to have worked out his flying machine.[1] They pick and eat juniper berries on a warm winter day or fruit from self-sown figs on a hot july one: or go on to the trattoría above Maiano, hamlet famous in sculpture, since Benedetto and Giuliano were born here,[2] Michelangelo was young here, and from nearby came the *pietra serena*, that creamy gentle grey stone used in fifteenth century capitals and corbels and ribs and groins. It is still so used; for masons hand-hew it out of the hills after blasts like cannon-bursts. There is one high quarry now disused where boys bathe in motionless water. It looks as deep as a volcano, and more than one bather has been drowned.

We remain, however, at the Via Verdi view, with all

[1] Actually Leonardo finished his twenty-seven-page treatise on the Flight of Birds in Paris toward the end of his life. His flying machine, to be worked by a man with wings, was never tried out and was founded on a misconception of the action of wings in flight. But much still remains to be revealed about this remarkable artist's scientific conclusions and inventions.

[2] These two brothers might have been numbered among the world's finest sculptors if they had not lived at a time and place with finer.

Florence's red-tiled roofs and ochreous walls below us. To the left the Chianti hills, usually blue though not far distant, rounded and opulent, proclaim unseen vineyards. To the right the Arno leads into the plain dominated by Monte Morello, Florence's own hill, a two-humped camel waiting on her. Further to the right from the house behind, the Apuan Alps can be seen near the invisible sea, always white but less with snow than with marble. And opposite you can trace the Viale dei Colli, a serpentine avenue vaulted with pines and columned with firs and cypresses, which was cut through fields and villa gardens in 1868 when Florence became the first and transient capital of the new Kingdom of Italy. Olives still grow between this avenue and the city centre, a bowshot from the Ponte Vecchio.[1] Florence is still a village.

The Viale dei Colli spreads out at one point of its course into the Piazzale Michelangelo, balancing across the city our little landing, and echoing the other serpentine road, on our side, which climbs up to Fiesole at the genial will of the Grand Duke Leopold who liked landscape and good farming. Stand on that Piazzale, and you reverse the view over Florence from the Apuan west over the Fiesole hills and through the dip north of the Chianti hills to the high Prato Magno, silver or gold or pink or grey by sun and season, the Great Meadow, a massif of rock which tops Vallombrosa (Milton stayed there) twenty and more miles away.

Most of these hills are not just scenery. They are part of florentine lives. They are as much the lungs of the city as the green squares of Bloomsbury and the Parks are the lungs of London. For in july and august the city centre is stifling. In

---

[1] Perhaps the most famous old bridge in the world. Tourists find its goldsmiths' shops quaint and rewarding. It was the only florentine bridge not blown up by the Germans during their retreat at the end of the last war, and the only one also to have survived the floods of six centuries, at least two of which were disastrous.

A few years ago, to save the structure, wheeled traffic was excluded by permanent posts placed at each end. The goldsmiths objected, thinking this would reduce trade. But it has increased it. Visitors can now move on the narrow pavements and cross from side to side as undistracted by motor cars and bicycles as if on the Rialto at Venice.

the evenings Florentines escape to the Piazzale for air. Sundays and holidays they spend in Fiesole, or in the woods of Borgunto beyond it, or by upland roadsides; or they lunch in outlying villas or farmsteads which have turned into restaurants.

Thousands of little ant-like cars (there are proportionately fewer big cars in Florence than in Rome or Milan), dust-grey or ivory (and recently some tomato-red), all shaped alike, shoot out from sideroads and chase each other like seconds to the minute up the roads to the hills. There is always the smart oaf in an Alfa-Romeo trying to break his own record from Piazza della Libertà to Monte Morello.

At these times there are more cars and children and lovers in the woods and glens than there are bushes of white-covered tree-heather. Monte Morello becomes Hampstead Heath. One solid car park with a noble view, which the Florentines stare at. Behind, the rich can hire horses and equitate in and out of couples in lanes.

The return after dark is more sober. People start up their cars at different hours of the morning; but they all steer home about the same hour for supper. Ants become slugs, moving a yard at a time. Tooting is forbidden. The shrill whistles of perspiring policemen, appointed to bottlenecks, pierce the patience of panting engines and humanity. All long for hot bed.

One benefit of this hubbub for health is that the Florentine knows his city also from above. Which is important for understanding it. You can make neither architectural nor historical sense of Florence by walking through her streets. They are too jumbled, too planless, six centuries, twenty centuries, roughly paraded together for identification. But from above, from the Via Verdi at Fiesole, you can make sense.

From under a parapet an olive grove falls away into the outskirts, with marrows and potatoes, unmown hay and scarlet poppies. A boy makes a *glissando* on pan pipes. He can be heard in the suburbs.

Florence is not a green city like Kiev nor a rock city like Edinburgh or Madrid. She lies like the bed of a drained lake with coloured stones left in patterns. Patterns are visible from up here.

Of the original Florence in the walls the Romans planned, where 5,000 people lived in wood and straw, a city state like Athens where craftsmen in wool voted by direct assembly, nothing remains. The city's aspect was changed by rich foreigners, the *Signorotti*, conquerors of land outside, who came down from their castles in the hills to lord it over the Florentines. They had strange northern names like Manzecca, Visdomini, Usimbardi. But already in the little shops[1] there was community sense. The rich ex-Franks or ex-Lombards, if they wished to exploit Florence, were compelled to abandon absenteeism and reside at least four months of every year within her walls. As each of them hated, feared and distrusted the others, they all built stone towers to live in. Very high towers. Some were over 200 feet high; and there came to be 150 of them. Early Florence was a baby New York.[2]

In the thirteenth century a second city emerged by a bourgeois revolution. The 30,000 dwellers in the little shops had marshalled themselves into 'Arts,' or as we would call them, Guilds. Everybody had to belong to one or another. Even Dante was at social law a druggist or apothecary, which meant he was supposed to know all about simples and maybe poisons. Membership soon became a form, like the worshipful tooth-pullers of London.

There were two classes inside these Arts: lawyers, merchants, doctors, money-changers, druggists, workers in wool, silk

---

[1] I use the word 'shop' to render *bottega*, which was both shop and workshop and home too. It was used of even the greatest artists' premises in our sense of 'studio.'

[2] For height, see the two leaning towers of Bologna: one is 320 feet and the unfinished one 156. For a general impression go to San Geminiano, southwest of Florence, which still has a few towers, though not so high. The London Monument is 202 feet high.

and fur, who were called the Fat Folk. And butchers, bakers, masons, vintners, who were called the Thin Folk. As yet there was no class war. They were united against their oppressors, the rich families in the tall towers. They forced down the height of the towers to under 90 feet, which was still high enough. They set up their own magistrates. By law the two chief ones had to be other than Florentine: for stubbornness with power became prudence, and the florentine spirit was beginning to appear: Go Your Own Way. With everyone beginning to go his own way, only an outsider could be respected.

The Fat Folk invented the golden Florin and became, individually, world bankers. They bejewelled themselves.

Florentines went their own ways in the sense that their cypresses do. A cypress needs all the goodness of its locality to stay where it is, and suffers little undergrowth round its feet.

Florentines grew jealous and mistrustful of each other. They too set up towers to live in, though not so tall as those of the *Signorotti*. You can trace the next city by these, now mostly six-storey piles of old stones flanked by younger buildings in almost every narrow street of the centre. In many you will notice dozens of square holes, as if stones had fallen out, but with corbels below, often finely moulded. These slots and tusks held beams for bridges between tower and tower, so that allied families could meet without going down into hostile streets. When any alliance collapsed, the beams were hastily removed, but the holes stayed open for the next alliance. They still do.

From the same façades strange iron hooks and rings protrude like a series of barren inn-signs. These were to hold poles on which to dry clothes, cloths and curtains. From the hooks were suspended on special occasions tapestries in an ebullience of the new fashion of display.

The highest tower of all is that of the Signoría. This is its proper name[1] because it was built as the premises of the Standard-Bearer of Justice and of the Priors of the Arts, by a new constitution which re-established order about a.d. 1300 This tower stands not on the ground but in the not quite centre of an irregular cube of stones from the Boboli quarries. Symmetry was not yet required. Function in locality was all. Architecturally the Signoría reaches over the Renaissance to our own day with our asymmetrical factories and houses. It is like a scientific apparatus made in the middle ages and still working. Push down the rod, and all Florence turns round the revolving gears.

The Signoría is still the centre of Florence. On feast days and holidays and when distinguished strangers are city guests, countless torches break into flame right up its walls at dusk. They flicker excitedly long after midnight, a form of flood-lighting even more impressive than Edinburgh Castle's. They seem from here on the Via Verdi like a heart that quivers among the still stars of the city lights.

Under the Signoría stand famous statues on the piazza. Every one of them is a protest against tyranny.

For the 80,000 people who now lived in the city, life was dangerous. The thin folk warred against the fat folk. The fat folk warred against themselves. This explains the business of the Guelphs and Ghibellines—despair of schoolboys.

The terms, I believe, come from the ambitions of a Duke of Bavaria, whose people instead of shouting 'Heil Hitler!' shouted 'Hi Welf!' the name of his uncle. The rival faction replied with 'Hi Weibling' the name of a swabian castle.

To simplify the european complications that sprang from this simple teutonic sport, we are told that the Ghibellines stood for the Holy Roman Emperor and the Guelphs for the Pope. If this were true a simonidean mnemonic would not be difficult, since one faction and its patron are trisyllabic and the

---

[1] Often called the Old Palace, because the Medici family governed from there before moving to the Pitti Palace when they were ennobled.

other mono. But history is not so easy as it is taught: and the split in Florence had little to do with Teutons or Tiaras. The 'noble' families of Florence, mostly now merchant bankers derived from the money-lenders of the Fat Folk, did side with the Pope when this suited their protection, and the rest of the Fat Folk, for protection against them, did look to the Emperor, whoever he happened to be. The jealousy and resentment of the Thin Folk toward all the Fat Folk made them side with their enemies' enemies. For the spirit of Florence was learning that to go your own way at all in even a nominal democracy you have to find others going the same way.

Civil war, or rather civil wars, were inevitable. As first one class and then another got the upper hand, or even groups inside classes, each murdered or exiled its opponents and always burned down their houses. In some decades of this, florentine architecture was in danger of extinction. The situation was saved for democracy (if I may so put it) during a very short period by a kind of proto-socialist dictatorship under a genius or madman of a patrician called Giani della Bella. He passed some just laws but did not understand his own revolution. He was sentenced to death by a part of the Guelphs, then excommunicated by the Pope, and then exiled. He died in Paris in 1311, the rich representative of the family bank of the Pazzis there.[1]

In a sense, each of the factions in this bloody period was fighting for freedom, at least for the freedom to expand, which implies the will to expand: a corollary of Going Your Own Way. Out of the turbidity expansion came clear, not only that of the bankers in their interests, but also that of the fingers in the little shops. Florence became a fashion centre. She seems to have invented coloured woollen stockings,

---

[1] The Pazzi family were later rivals of the Medici family. They tried to assassinate two leading Medicis during the concentrated silence of the congregation at the Elevation of the Host during Mass in the Cathedral. Lorenzo de' Medici escaped and his revenge for the murder of his brother practically exterminated the rival family.

just as later she covered buttons with the same cloth as they were sewn into. That is why today ladies in Florence can buy the most elegant shoes in Europe at high prices from famous makers who live and work here; but also others, no less elegant and costing less, from the very hands that fashioned them in a back room.

Expansion brought riches and personal power. The great family of the Rucellai, for example, takes its name from their *Orto degli Oricelli*, or Orchil Patch, where they grew a certain lichen from which they made a secret dye, base of the family fortune. It was in this garden that the Platonic Academy[1] continued to meet for a while after the downfall of the Medicis. When the Medicis returned to power, the garden was wrecked, but later restored; and part of it can still be seen from a side-street between the railway station and Porta al Prato.

Florence's sense of community expanded too. Under her many tyrants, gentle or cruel or both together, wise, cunning or ineffectual, she learned that to go your own way you have also to provide for others. She set up the first public ambulance system in the world. Perhaps the first public hospital in a real sense. One of the earliest academies of art. She had the first paved streets and squares since roman times. Later came the first botanic garden. The corridor in the Medici offices (*Uffizi*) was to give the word 'Gallery' to any room in the world which exhibits pictures.

Symbol of this expanding enterprise is the great red strawberry of Brunelleschi's Dome, triumph of collective engineering. From our lookout it dwarfs everything else. In the late light it seems to tilt a trifle backward, as if always astonished at the setting sun: an optical illusion, for it is structurally

---

[1] Founded by Cosimo de' Medici, and developed by Lorenzo. The italian Renaissance might not have been what it was if this collection of first-class brains had never met for discussion as a kind of gingergroup for artists and patrons. It had no premises but met in the gardens of country houses where the chief Medici was staying.

The 'secret dye' is not improbable. Orchil turns red or blue like litmus paper; and in those days of scant chemical experimentation the blends of acid and alkali could well have been kept a family secret.

perfect. This is supported by the lesser and later strawberries of San Lorenzo, San Frediano and other churches. Round it spreads the third city (or fourth, if you count the roman): the Florence of the Renaissance, the merchant bankers, super-craftsmen, statesmen with their famous names: Medici, Strozzi, Pazzi, Bardi, Peruzzi, Rucellai, Guicciardini. You can meet their descendants at parties, one improbable surname following another as its owner announces it in the italian fashion of introduction, with a slight bow.

These built their *palazzi* for beauty more than defence: and it does not matter much even to the purist that the top storey of the Palazzo Rucellai is a mere curtain wall with nothing behind. The principles discovered in the building of these became models for France and Austria, England and Denmark, Scotland, Ireland and the United States. Till they became conventions not principles, and wore themselves out.

The outlines of this city, three times bigger than its predecessor, are clear. Where the great walls ran, now wide avenues follow, crowded with cars and lorries and even a few double-decker buses, and columned with planes, horse-chestnuts, limetrees that in june you scent before you see. Many of the great gates in these walls are left in isolation where the high roads radiated out of the inflated centre, Porta al Prato, Porta San Gallo, Porta Romana: not beautiful, faintly chinese, their historical functions gone.

Outside this circumvallation swells nineteenth and twentieth century Florence: shuttered, plaster-faced suburban flats with terraces or balconies, houses with gardens, growing workers'-tenements to east and west. In one sense it was good that the capital of Italy passed from Turin to Rome. Capitals sprout factories overnight. The hills of Florence would have been as black with smoke and chimneys as Sheffield's. Better in flattened Rome with its perennial water supply. As she stands, Florence has few factories. Her prosperity comes still from the fingers of her little people.

34

At night the drained lake seems to fill again, and the stars in streets and window swim as in water. Down to your right are coloured sky signs, over the hideous Piazza della Repubblica, formerly named after the King, seat of banks and tourists' cafés, near the superannuated Post Office. This square could well be in Brussels or Paris or London. It has no character. But it stands openly where slums and ghetto had closed over the old roman forum, where the approaching streets still run along as through the *porta decumana* and the *porta praetoria*.[1] Just off the pavement there is a pillar, a nuisance to both pedestrians and traffic. It carries a statue of Abundance. Part of the pillar, original roman, stood on this site.

Abundance. A florentine quality. We will follow this out more fully another day. Meantime, where we stand, an etruscan sentry may well have stood, looking down at the tiny torchlights of the new power by the river. For us now it is hard to tell which are fixed lights on hills and which fixed stars above them. For him there would be no fixed lights on the hills. But maybe fireflies winked green round him as they do round us, one sitting on my shoulder as we turn to go in.

---

[1] Roman terms for the principal camp gate turned away from the expected enemy, and for the gate facing the enemy, respectively. Roman 'camps' were not encampments under canvas but walled forts round which in time grew cities whose names in Britain often end in –chester.

4 ❦

The Fireflies

'It is indeed a most wonderful view' said the swedish lady. The german lady, watercolouring it, agreed. The german lady's husband stood behind her at the parapet and looked.

'Most beautiful' sighed the german lady up and down the lemonade sky, the eau-de-nil, the red mullet clouds in aspic.

'I stay here' said the swedish lady.

The german lady's husband looked.

'Do you stay down there?' the german lady brushed at cottages plunging away in difficult perspective.

'O no' said the swedish lady indulgent. 'I stay in a *pensione* higher up. The view from my window is indescribable.'

'It would be nice' said the german lady 'to live down there.' Her husband considered the cottages and preferred the view.

Gravel stepped jimply down between wall and cottages, a slim log of white stone limiting each level of doorway. Pansies, marigolds, sweet william, small sweet peas. Rambler roses grouped the doors into a pink colonnade.

'Especially' said the german lady, 'that little house down at the end.'

The little house at the bottom had the best garden. Here the path terraced itself out for roses pink, crimson, white and yellow; for a big stone washing-trough; for a huge blue umbrella sprouting up from an old grindstone.

'A sad house' said the swedish lady, imparting resident's knowledge. 'Little Sabinetta there had encephalitis. It has left a lesion of the brain. She cannot recover.'

The german lady, asking if that was the mother, was told,

No, the parents were away in another city up north, where they lived. The illness of the child, said the swedish lady, aweing her voice, came between them. 'When they come, they squabble all day. We hear them from my *pensione*.'

'The deaths of children' said the german lady in sincere rebuke, choosing a different paint, 'do so often, I have observed.' Her husband moved a foot nearer to compare the new colour with the old mountains.

'At night also' said the swedish lady in contented mastery, 'the lights of the city lie down there like, like, just like jewels. And the *lucciole*, they come up till you would think the city itself were rising.'

'*Lucciole*? What is that?' asked the german lady's husband, who turned out to be abrupt.

'Fireflies' said his wife. He returned to his looking.

Swallows swooped on the street, deft gentlemen of the first empire in dark-blue and white.

The Signora Lisi chanted '*One*-two three, *Four*-five six, *Seven*-eight-nine' bouncing Sabinetta like a boat on a high waltz at the culmination of *Twelve!* 'Smile, please' she commanded, and teased the corners of Sabinetta's mouth till it came, pleased and slightly coquettish.

Sabinetta had floss-soft pale-gold hair. She had a luminous skin, which stretched over her fine cheekbones the distinction of an adult. Her limbs were tunes without false notes, though her legs did not stand and her wrists were twisted one back one forward like half a swastika.

Her splendid eyes brimmed wonder and tenderness, and their squint in no way blemished them. That she turned up her head to heaven as if the nape pulled tighter than the throat in no way impaired her naturalness. She seemed to be enjoying a silent laugh. She had much charm. She had no brain.

The Signora Lisi, like all the villagers, loved Sabinetta. The Signora Lisi's husband had been killed by Germans in his appennine village. Her only daughter was in a mental hospital. The Signora Lisi let lodgings to foreigners and was so fond that when each departed all became saints in her account of them. Even Germans.

The Signora Lisi had been a sweet tough peasant girl. She had learnt to grow rough and coarse and cunning. She never cheated her tenants, because she chose them. She chose their rent too, by their clothes and the look in their eyes. She chose all the goods she bought in shops, because she could not afford to buy a bad tomato.

She scorned to report her tenants to the *Comune*[1], until an enemy denounced her. Then she had to pay more in arrears of sojourn tax than she took in one summer. This she lamented loudly all up the street and down the little path to whoever would listen. Neighbours said it served her right for being mean: and hurried themselves to report one of their many tenants.

Sabinetta was by far the favourite of all the tenants she had ever had. She conspired with Sabinetta's nurse to water her with words as if intelligence might germinate. They crooned and talked and invited her to talk.

But Sabinetta, as both knew, could no more talk than walk. She bubbled and coughed and howled like a newborn.

The Signora Lisi knew, as the nurse never told her, that Sabinetta could not live. Which stunned her eyes sometimes. Which folded round her mouth. Which she concealed from Sabinetta in case Sabinetta might guess.

Sabinetta grew worse. She stopped sleeping. She stopped eating. She was vomiting. Her weight fell and her skin went wax. There were hollows round her eyes, blue as mountains. Then she died.

The father came to take her away. The nurse wrote to the Signora Lisi about the funeral. Sabinetta having been baptised when she was born, said the priest, there was no danger for

[1] Local government administration.

her soul, which, said the priest, having once been created was indestructible, doing now the will of God like all other indestructible souls, even though she had no brain, said the priest.

The Signora Lisi sat under the empty umbrella after the sun set. Her hands were folded on the invisibling letter. She wept in the dark.

The fireflies came. Rising out of the ilex trees, small green lamps that flashed and grew bigger as they arrived, like messages; signalling surely and evenly, leaping and swimming where they wished, pulses of a single bloodstream, green, hidden in black.

As if content that in their existence lay their purpose.

One came down on the knee of the Signora Lisi. A small insect, undistinguished, like a weevil. To her a tiny, alternating light.

5

Abundance

Abundance is less than opulence but more than plenty. Florence is not a great city, but it abounds. About the same size as Sheffield, (500,000 inhabitants), she may be less or more wealthy, I do not know. Nor do I much care, not using 'abundance' in that sense. However, if you ask in Sheffield for a particular type of knife which is out of stock, you must wait till an anonymous middleman pleases to supply one: if you ask in Florence for a particular type of leather-clad box or vellum-backed book, the shopkeeper himself is quite capable of making one for you that evening, and will do so if you are in a hurry. This abundance of making is essentially florentine. It reduces millions of tons of steel rods or molten metal swinging through the air in great bucketfuls (despite the brains and resources that go into that and the national charges that come out of it) to an impersonal process of mere melting.

This from the visitor's angle, of course: and visitors should be canny with their judgments. One has to know so much before one sees anything.

Where centuries of abundance have crystallised in social forms, it is easier for the visitor sometimes to be mistaken by not seeing. Plain and dismal florentine streets should not be dismissed as slums or commercial quarters. Inside a portal a portico may lead to a fine square garden with tall trees, winding paths, big vases of blossoming shrubs and even flowerbeds. Zinnias, callas, giant pansies, stocks. There is sure to be a statue or at least an ornamental urn of terracotta from

Impruneta, which has supplied such beautifications since the fourteenth century: not museum pieces but in character with the place: positions rather than objects of art. Such gardens lead us to suppose that there was some truth in the notion that Florence was called a City of Flowers, as today is visible only from an aeroplane.

Florence decorates herself publicly, with flowers in street islands and the middles of avenues. Most modern cities do that, even if not all have statues parting the traffic, a bronze fawn or a pony like a ship's figurehead. But her abundance strews streets with petals for the processions on Corpus Domini Day, as it has done since this feast was first instituted in the thirteenth century.

With faith, as with flowers. Few are the shops that do not have a miniature Madonna high up on the wall, in various materials and varying taste, lit by a glow-worm electric bulb. This is as functional in its sense as the now unnecessary notice against spitting: but something is added as well. Many are the street corners with stone Madonnas in niches. Not rare are painted or frescoed ones, some of beauty, now glassed-in for protection. Protestants need not be irritated by this abundance of Madonnas, and presbyterians might well reconsider the grim frugality of their own faith. One does not resent the fountains of Rome; and I imagine that to spiritual people a Madonnina in a florentine street can be as refreshing as blossom of sweet water.

The faith of most Florentines today, I would venture, is more that of Lorenzo de' Medici than that of Savonarola. The life that has always been much as it still is, comes first; the goodness of God is in eternity. A realistic rather than a mystical attitude to the Deity. This may be seen in the myriad *presepi* that are prepared in the home and in the church at Christmas. These are groups of model figures round a scene representing the Nativity. The stable and manger may be made of anything from an old box to a priceless baroque work of art. There are all the correct personages: the Holy Family, the shepherds, the Wise Men, together with sheep, and ox, and ass. But outside, the scene is often extended with moss for moor or pasture, and half-hidden mirrors for pool on which ducks float, dogs drink, fishermen fish. All kinds of characters may be added in all kinds of styles and scales, even little japanese people, or figures from any other part of the world where the head of the house has travelled. A sort of private summary of a public world, an abundant overspill of personal celebration.[1]

In the first *presepe* I ever saw, and the most famous in Florence, dimly lit, childlike and reverent at once, the atmosphere was shredded by a sharp nasal voice whining from a gramophone record which crackled, in american-english, that it was anticipating a white Xmas.

Even the dead receive their abundance. Toward All Saints' and All Souls' Days the single-decker trolleybuses double their time-table to Trespiano. On the Day of the Dead itself there is no time-table; for buses leave as soon as they fill up. Trespiano is a long village straggling up the slope which launches the directest road from Florence to Bologna over the Appennines. For miles round can be seen its burialground, white and walled like an arab city, Florence's chief cemetery. It is incumbent on all bereaved to visit their dead on the eve of, or on, their day; and many people take two bunches of flowers, one for their own dead, the other for any grave or tomb unvisited.

The very young get special abundance at Epiphany and Carneval. After the gifts and joys of eleven of the days of Christmas, which, because school holidays are short, are crammed with children's parties, Epiphany comes as another feast with more gifts—slighter gifts because the family gift funds are depleted. The day when the baby Jesus was shown

[1] Pious people visit seven *presepi* at Christmastime, as they visit seven Entombments at Easter.

to the Magi has become in Florence an old woman with a broom. Not a witch, though she resembles one, she dates from some mysterious supernatural figure which in pagan times went about distributing gifts for six days on earth and vanished on the seventh—now the 6th of january. That night the chimney-piece is lined with red paper after the children have gone to bed. In centrally heated flats a table is spread. In the morning there are minor gifts on the red paper, sweets, trinkets, toy guns, or the little model motor cars made as solidly as a moon rocket by a firm of british toymakers.

But if a child has been consistently naughty, the Befana brings them only a lump of coal.

The compassion of modern manufacture and commerce has now produced a lump of coal which is in fact made of sugar.

The presence of the Befana can be felt throughout the year. In some families when a milk tooth comes out, it is wrapped in paper with the Befana's name written on it and placed on the hearth or table. In the morning there lies a small coin. For the Befana has no teeth at all and pays willing reward for her comforts.

As a matter of mythological fact the Befana has strayed in from Carneval (and into Carneval from centuries ago), being the Old Woman who in crude folk plays was executed by the populace together with her jolly husband the Old Year, who became Carneval. In this form she was a lifesize puppet, which when sawn in two burst into a largesse rain of nuts and dried figs. In the fifteenth century each of the florentine Arts made its own Old Woman; but a specially bountiful communal one was also hung from a ladder and sawn up in the Mercato Nuovo.[1]

Further communal munificence occurs at mid-Lent public dances and festivities, when a large earthenware pot called

---

[1] The second and penultimate public food market of Florence: visitors now buy straw bags and tablemats and holiday headgear and gewgaws there.

the *Pentolaccia*[1] is hung from a high ceiling, and blindfolded young men try to batter it with long poles. The game becomes a romp because each striker gallops across the unseen floor to avoid being brained by lumps of pottery and cascading prizes if he strikes lucky. Even Lent, which many Florentines observe, cannot smother abundance.

Within living memory small boys used to fix little paper ladders on unaware ladies' backs at mid-Lent, but I have not seen this done. Carneval is not what it was anywhere in Italy, not even in Venice, where on the morning after mid-Lent there are no hangovers, no traces of saturnalia nor indeed of vanished crowds, except a few handfuls of confetti lying in corners, probably thrown by children.

Carneval has passed to the children, more so than Christmas; and again they break out in parties. At these, confetti by request of parents and maids is replaced with coloured streamers. But confetti used to be the focus of multicoloured Carneval. At first the word meant confectionery, sweets wrapped in paper for throwing. It was then applied to the paper itself, cut in tiny pieces for throwing. In Britain it has retained this single meaning, and the nineteenth century coined the word 'comfit' for the sugar-coated almonds which are still called *confetti* in italian. These are produced in a big bowl at all weddings, rich or poor, and three or five are sent to friends or relatives unable to be present. In rich families these few relics of the Old Woman slain for abundance are enclosed in more lasting material than paper: salt-cellars, ash-trays, pots, of silver or fine china.

The children still look forward eagerly to Carneval. The smaller ones go to school or kindergarten in fancy dress and masks. And along the Lungarno[2] between parked cars a few

---

[1] Meaning 'Rotten' or 'Scrap' Pot. Maybe originally old and cracked pots were hung up.

[2] The name given to the streets on both banks of the Arno, divided into sections named after prominent buildings in them or (in later extensions) after prominent Florentines. At one end it is possible to park a car without being lucky.

hawkers still set out barrows with (our) confetti, masks, drums, toffee, balloons and cardboard trumpets. The broom of the Befana is now used only by maggiordomos patiently sweeping coloured dots out of rich doorways along the river.

On Ascension Day in Old Russia people used to release caged birds in an abundance of gratitude for the earthly life of Jesus. Pushkin wrote a poem about it. In Florence on Ascension Day nearly everyone goes to the Cascíne.

The Cascíne were meadows by the river which were turned into a public park in the eighteenth century. There had been a dairy farm in them to supply the Medici household with milk and cream for the family, staff, courtiers, hangers-on, artists, bodyguard, grooms and visiting princes. All kinds of trees were planted there: elms, white poplars, holm-oaks, conifers. It is said that Shelley in 1818 wrote his *Ode to the West Wind* there. If this is true, it is strange. A West Wind is rare in Florence, the usual winds being the *Tramontana* from the north, the south-east damp *Scirocco*, and the fierce *Libeccio* from Libya in the south, which blows the windows open. Also to a poet wandering in the Cascíne evergreen trees are more noticeable than deciduous ones.

Certainly the poem was written in the year during which Shelley was in Italy; and there may be a deeper personal meaning in the abused last line: *If winter comes, can Spring be far behind*? For the Shelleys had just lost their second child and Mary gave birth to the third in Florence: for which reason he was called Percy Florence Shelley.[1] But it was the north wind, not the west, which drove the weak-lunged poet on medical advice to the warmer climate of Pisa.

However, trees there certainly are in the Cascíne for leaves to fall from, yellow and pale and hectic red, if seldom perhaps

---

[1] The young father probably did not know that there was a precedent for the maleness of the name in an eleventh century monk at Worcester. Two years later the parents of Florence Nightingale also named a child after the city where it was born, from which it became a girl's name internationally. Percy Florence Shelley later succeeded to the family baronetcy.

black: and between and under them on Ascension Day stall-keepers cry all manner of goods for sale from funny hats to carpets and family tables. Unlike the Borghese Gardens in Rome, which are mounded, the Cascíne are flat as Romney Marsh, with fields of coarse grass partitioned by straight wide avenues. Six months after the floods of november 1966 these fields were still mud and puddle: but that did not stop Ascension Day merrymakers from breaking through hedges or vaulting rows of iris to get into them; for here as usual was all the fun of the fair, roundabouts of many kinds, swings, giant wheel, motorcar bumps and those quiet games of chance which only the proprietor, curiously, ever wins.

On the main avenue sucking-pigs are roasting, because the traditional dish is *porchetta*, stuffed with garlic and rosemary. Most people eat walking and drink at cleanly stalls, but there are one or two impromptu trattorías under the trees. If there is a thunderstorm, as frequently there is, canvas awnings are stretched, full of holes, and diners move from one splashed table to pack another. This adds to friendliness.

If it is fine, one is soon hard put to move along the avenues, so thick are the families strolling hand in hand as Florentines do on festival days, or piled with parcels. Every child has a gas-filled balloon, globular or duck-shaped or elephant-trunk-shaped, many of which escape skyward as the hours pass. One sees few tears at such losses. There can be tears if the children themselves get lost; for there is no lost-children or first-aid tent, though police cars slowly patrol the avenues. But in abundance there is bound to be loss and confusion.

Goldfish are on sale in tiny plastic bags of water, and rabbits, puppies, tortoises and cagebirds. But the principal purchases of the day are miniature houses of wood-chip and wire with crickets inside. Vendors have big boxes of crickets, which boys have been grubbing for in long grass. The bottom of the box looks like the inside of a bee-skip. With seemingly expert fingers the vendors feel among the swarming black-brown bodies, and choose you your cricket as a good singer, which may or may not be an expert judgment. And the children carry their lodgers home in the little houses (not all are dwellingplaces: they can have more up-to-date ones shaped like petrol stations), hoping they will chirrup all night. As some of them do. Next morning the children release them. With little thought of Ascensions.

This day is called Ascension Day only in church circles. To Florentines it is the Festival of the Cricket; and they are trying to smarten it up with a morning procession headed by a gigantic Cricket like the old Carneval floats, and with afternoon concerts of popular music. Such improvements have always been being made in popular festivals. They will hardly alter the character of this one. The conflicts of shrieking jazz records and squealing voices on loudspeakers all too close from all too near roundabouts are no more raucous or un-pleasing than the rigid blasts of rival calliopes in older days. I do not think much can be taken away. There will still be the men with working models of florentine tradesmen turned by a handle, made who knows how many years ago for a gift of five *centesimi* from a passerby. There have been such for generations at this festival: the city's spiritual vent and relaxation in spring, the only feastday when working Florentines stay in Florence.

How to Drive a Car in This Country

'Hope you're a good driver' he said, pulling his raincoat over his knees and slamming the passenger door too violently; 'No place for a beginner, Italy. When I first came here, couldn't make head or tail of it.

'This precedence given to traffic from the right: perfectly absurd in this country with its left-hand drive. Means the driver can't see the traffic coming in from the right through his passenger's head, eh?

'Means at a crossroads everyone has to give way to everyone else. At peak hours that's a solid traffic jam with four tangents. Needs a policeman to sort out every crossroads. And there never is a policeman. Or not if it's raining.

'Now they're putting up more and more traffic-lights. But all set, all automatic, no variation with the flow. Result, more chaos, see what I mean?

'But if it's you coming in from the right, do they give you precedence? Not they! They accelerate and call at you. Dreadful fellows for calling! Even the main roads don't have precedence, town or country: not unless they have those diamond signs you can't see 'cos the trees hide 'em. Then you find you're in a section of the same road where the precedence has stopped, which you can't see till you've had it. Crash, smash, calling and chaos again.

'All right you've got precedence far as you can see. Never

48

trust it! A *moto* will jump at you like a viper. Know what a *moto* is? A motor-assisted push-bike with the speed of a Maserati ridden by a child of fifteen. No licence needed. Sounds like a circular saw in knotty wood. Hardly any brakes and can't stop in a hundred yards. Young bodies diving across your bonnet like porpoises.

'Hope your brakes are good, we're coming to a roundabout.

'Roundabouts are new here. These people can't understand 'em. No more can I, in this country. Look, you're coming in here from the right and you want to go left. You have the precedence, so signal with your flickerer, that's right. Not one of 'em taking any notice, see what I mean? All of 'em flickerering all different, one left, one right there, one going on. There you are: traffic jam!

'Soon as it's sorted out, you'll see! Round to the left, that's it. There's cars coming in from the right and overtaking you, they've the right to. There's cars coming in from the left, lots of 'em: they haven't but they do. There's another lot from that sidestreet. There's several on your tail. Look left, look right, look behind on both sides—look out, man! Blimey, a woman pushing a pram on the crossing in this maelstrom! And she's a right to. Need six pairs of eyes, you do, eight pairs, see what I mean?

'Rome's worse. Free for all there. Milan's all traffic lights and traffic lanes and they slide over the lot. Genoa's too mean to do street-repairs; toss you on the pavement. Naples I've never bin to, I'ld die of driving. Best place in Italy for cars is Venice, see what I mean?

'Course, there are good things in this country: some. Kerb-parked cars all facing the same way. Good that; different when you go through France or back to old England. Higgledy-piggledy there. Cars crossing two ways like geese. Not so here, you know. Park your car wrong side of the road, like I did once when the petrol pipe blocked. Left it all night. Arrested by the Maresciallo of the *carabinieri* in person next morning. But you can sort that out here if you're a foreigner. Good fellow the Maresciallo. Came for a drink afterwards. They know everyone's ignorant in this country. Nobody reads the new highway code any more. They fine for the old offences. Or if you cheek 'em.

'Parking's a problem, 'course. So it is in all countries. Doing their best, I suppose. No room here. Office-wallahs leave their cars parked all day. Perfectly absurd! Ought to have more buses and smaller, more taxis and cheaper, and keep all cars out.

'Cars used to be pleasure when I was young. Now they're just a means of not getting about. Good, that, eh?

'Then these zones of silence, perfectly absurd! Historical, you know. Mussolini imposed 'em, I'm told, 'cos the Eye-ties tooted too much, like the Frenchies. After they'd shot him, I'm told, you never heard such a din everywhere. Had to be reimposed. But it won't ever work, not in Florence. All them twisty walled lanes on the outskirts. Hundreds. Not allowed to sound your horn, perfectly absurd. And don't be taken in if you do hear a pip-pip like a prewar pushbike round the corner. Like as not it's a ten-ton lorry with a trailer filling the lane.

'These autostradas now: boring. Know Italy invented the autostrada, did you? From Milan to the Lakes. Three lanes. Most dangerous road in Europe. Widened it now. But I must say them autostradas make our motorways look amateur, see what I mean? Restaurants here, snackbars there, repair shops, petrol stations every few miles and no speed limit. And the warnings of fog or ice, wonderful!

'Trouble is, come back to it, the way they drive. Too fast for their own control often as not. Dart out, nip in, can't take corners. Dozens of deaths. Trouble is, they've no regard for human life, their own nor yours. Fast as they can for as far as they can and jam on the brakes. Collision? Other man's fault!

Off again, fast as they can for as far as they can and jam on the brakes. Tail another car close up as possible, tagging his exhaust: jam on the brakes. Corners? Traffic-lights? Traffic-signs? Accidents? Never look out for 'em, never anticipate! When I learned to drive I was taught to anticipate everything.

'Kind of a sort of gives you a pain in the neck sort of thing, see what I mean?

'I know it's their way of driving, that's what I'm saying. They get away with it. Perfectly absurd.

'Well, thanks for the lift, old man, and for the talk. See you next wednesday at the Consul's Party for Her Majesty's Birthday?'

'All the same, old boy, them lorry-drivers can't half manipulate them lorries.'

7

Spirit and Locality

It is glib and perilous to generalise about groups of people as types of people: dour Scots, jolly Jack Tars, correct Germans, decadent peons. One gets mawkish from ignorance or liverish from dislike or contempt. But one who lives in two countries can draw some distinctions in a general way. These derive from locality.

Of locality I have written in full elsewhere. It is a passage in time and space where history, geography, tradition and antitradition, parenthood, art, even (in the Soviet Union) class, and many other factors combine in each individual including those who rebel against locality. So one group of people can differ radically from another.

These groups are usually nations or groups of nations. In the italian nation there are sub-nations in the sense that Texans are not New Yorkers in the United States of America. The Genovese are as different from the Neapolitans as the Sicilians from the Alpini. Even the educated classes and the nobility speak among themselves dialects as mutually unintelligible to outsiders, almost, as scots from cockney. To folk from other cities or from abroad they speak standard italian, as Celts speak standard english, sometimes with a difference of consonants or lilt.

As a result any city can find itself dubbed by the others with derogatory epithets or jingles.

> *Torinese*
> *falso e cortese*
>
> (A man from Turin
> Has good manners to take you in).

Genova is mean. The people of Cuneo like those of Gotham are all born fools. And so on.

Florentines are supposed to be the biggest swearers in Italy.

There is some historical evidence for this. In the late middle ages so much blasphemy was heard in the streets that it was decided to exact a small fine for each swear-word. The money so accumulated in a short time was enough to found the *Misericordia*, the first public ambulance system in the world, and to equip it with two waggons. Before long a *loggia* was built[1] for a brigade station near the Duomo, which is still there, though now not big nor handy enough for its number of motor ambulances. The oaths continued. They still do.

Porca miseria! Porca l'oca! (= Lousy Hell!) are mild and meaningless expletives. *Madonna!* or *Madonna mia* (with the double —n— groaned out twice its length) are frequent alternatives, often disguised as *Mamma mia!* But when an amalgam of the adjective and noun is made, as to say 'Lousy Jesus', ears do not have to be stuffy to be offended. And there are many others, physical and uninhibited, more offensive yet to sensitive ones.

Florentines do not have the monopoly of these expressions; but it may be true that they are distributed over more classes and categories than is usual in other cities.

Florentines do not trouble to speak standard Italian unless it is useful in their work, and not always then. Having learned that standard Italian was founded on tuscan, largely by Dante's example, and that Dante loathed all other dialects especially roman, many speak their own broad aspirated speech to everyone.

This is due partly to history,—Florence having been the financial centre of Italy—; and partly to geography, because

---

[1] A loggia is an arcade on the ground floor at the front of a house, or looking on a garden. It can be either built-in or built-on; or an independent building as here. A terrazza on the ground floor (as few are) would be called a loggia only if it had some architectural pretensions, as, an arcade.

Florence lies half-way between north and south. The north despises the south: the poor south goes to the rich north to find work or assassinate some fugitive betrayer of a sister's or daughter's honour. Both south and north regard the Florentines as reserved, cold, smooth and provincial.

Having seen from our view on the hill something of what history has made of them, and from sharing in their festivities something of their natural abundance, let us now try to get to know them better, and see what grounds there may be for this unwelcome reputation.

One can well understand it. Florence is a small city. Business men do not spend in traffic jams an hour or so of their two free middleday hours. They spend more time at home than the Milanese. They do not dine in restaurants like the Romans day after day. There is little languishing in hot public shade or into the cooling night as further south. Almost all florentine cafés and bars close at midnight and most restaurants earlier. For Florentines entertain in their homes behind closed shutters or in floodlit but walled gardens under pallidescent cypresses. But entertain they do, and well, some formally, others with their jackets off, till the small hours of the morning.

Their houses are by comparison with other cities plainly furnished. Sparsely indeed, as befits industrious people's houses. The bourgeoisie has few knick-knacks or idle ornaments, the rich and noble have a few select masterpieces, a statue, cassapanca, escritoire in the exact centre of a wall. This seems chilly to british visitors, for whose ability to make any sort of a house into a comfortable home the Florentines have great envy.

Climate affects. It forbids carpets from corner to corner. Floors are of tile, or marble or brick, on which british feet clatter or squeak selfconsciously. For ventilation, ceilings tend to be high, making echoes too stately for british voices. It is easier to keep plants indoors than to grow flowers for cutting in the garden: and dozens of these fill corners and tables: ferns,

54

sansevieria, cactus, rubber plants of countless varieties. When it rains, most house-holders have flocks of pot-plants driven out on the terrazza, to be readmitted when the sun shines. These relieve the sparseness.

There is something of the renaissance palazzo in every florentine flat however modest: and when you get used to this, you no more notice it or feel apart than you would have as a friend of Lorenzo de' Medici. For there is something of the renaissance prince in every Florentine's makeup, however restricted. If you are his friend, he will protect and advise you within his powers as he would not do to another Florentine just because he was florentine. In his palazzo of a flat there is still something also of a tower.

Florentines have none of the commercial affability of the Milanese, the elegance of Turin, the ebullience of Naples. But I have not found them reserved. I have found them dignified. As some Scots are. As they have always been. As their architecture shows: rejecting the false top-show of writhing baroque, preferring at all periods harmonious proportion, which always accompanies self-respect.

They grumble about other Florentines, as they grumble about Florence: but Florence is what unites them all. The workers and lower middleclass have many sentimental songs about her, some funny ones, some richly ribald ones. Educated folk are proud of her in a quiet way as the centre of a kingdom without a king. They go for holidays to learn the world, but Florence remains their city with no equal. For Florence is to them all not beauty but people.

As for the nobles, they are not like their venetian peers, skimmed by two gondoliers in livery from palace to palace, nose in air. In Florence they work. They have fashion or export businesses, they make wines, they enter the learned professions, train horses, run organisations for tourism or the poor, write books, stand for Parliament. They are part of the city's life, even if like all aristocrats they keep themselves largely to their like. They are as proud of their city as of their family. But for them too it is not the beauty that counts.

If this is being provincial, it is provincial like Cataluña or Provence, and not like inferior-feeling individuals who want to go to Moscow or to make good in London.

Cold they certainly are not. No people who depend on tourists would survive if they were. But Florence was not founded by tourism and has not been changed by it. A populace governed by soldiers must become to a great extent military: a populace governed by merchants and bankers becomes sensitive to credit. It cannot be dishonest and it welcomes strangers of any nation including its own. It is likely to become shrewd but not smooth. People in need of credit avoid smooth customers. Florentines are friendly.

Our first friend here was a publisher, on whom we had called looking for work. A few days later he came to see us with some translation to be done and an invitation to his house for supper.

Later he took us to a restaurant near the Signoría, where later still we returned one evening by ourselves, being hungry. Translators do not earn much, and I tumbled out on the table all the money in my pocket. It was little. But we were given a full meal with wine and bread and extras like *grissini*[1]; and we have a special welcome every time we go back.

Nobody should judge a city's people only by the categories with whom visitors are principally in contact: waiters, bar-proprietors, shopkeepers. Good manners, as everyone knows, are good for trade. But the more closely one knows such people in Florence, the more one sees that this is not their chief motive. They are interested, or if you like inquisitive, about their clients. They like people and wish

---

[1] Those sticks halfway between bread and biscuit which used to be stuck in a tumbler but are now served in cellophane. Usually they are paid for in the cover charge which in snob restaurants is a ticket of entrance to the Royal Enclosure.

to share. That is why the Signora Lena called me 'Signor Giuseppe.'

And this cannot be called familiarity. It is the Italian's natural freedom. But they too have their share of florentine dignity. The result can be a gently wry wit.

Newly come to one trattoria, we praised the first course. 'My wife made it,' answered the waiter, who was also the proprietor. We praised the second course. We were quite sincere. 'My wife made it.' We saw him looking at us from time to time across the tables. Toward the end of our meal he brought his small daughter to be presented. 'My wife made this too' he said.

There are as many honest men in Florence as in Bristol. In eleven years I have only once been cheated. But many foreigners, especially Americans from the United States, have an almost neurotic fear of being cheated, which is not limited to their travels in Italy. A young american couple were running short of petrol in the country near Florence and asked for 20 litres at a wayside filling station, from the middle-aged woman who came to the pump. After some miles more they ran right out of petrol. It was some months before they could take that road again, and then they stopped to have the matter out, all the rectitude of Uncle Sam boiling in the young husband. Hardly had his recriminations begun, when the proprietor at the pump beamed with pleasure.

'*Ecco!* It was you! I am so glad. My wife was working the pump that day and is not good at it. She gave you 2 litres not 20. We didn't know how to find you and felt badly about it. Of course 18 litres are yours, with so many apologies, eh?'

There was no doubt of his sincerity.

If renaissance locality makes the descendants of craftsmen and the epigonoi of bankers self-reliant, it also continues another line from the chaos we saw from the hill.

Florentines have stopped stabbing each other during the

Elevation or in dark streets. They no longer burn down the houses of those they don't like. Street fights are rare and riots rarer, the latter usually engineered by para-political parties with small followings. Men, and women, do squabble in public sometimes, as you find in all cities of the world. Here there are no brandishing of knives, though there may be of fists. Bystanders watch, then go their own ways. Nevertheless Florentines of today are as much the lawbreakers they were in the time of Benvenuto Cellini[1]—with a different target.

The law has been a thing imposed on them for centuries, as on most of Italy, by flunkeys of foreign kings and emperors. When Italy became a kingdom in the nineteenth century, her civil, penal and procedural laws had, unfortunately, to be codified like, in their time, those of the new France, some of the american colonies, Frederick's Prussia. They were drawn up more for the lawyers than for the people. Mussolini's were drawn up more for his fascists than for the people, and these are still in force, under revision since 1942.

No civil case in Florence (and probably in other italian cities) comes to court under six months or a year. A criminal trial takes two years to prepare and can continue for several years after judgment. To go to court you need money: and more to get out of it. So the law to the citizen seems less a protection than a rod. Which is why he breaks it.

I do not refer to professional criminals. They are many. There can be as many as a dozen homicides on a newspaper page in one day in Italy. A proportion of these is tuscan, a proportion of that florentine. Sometimes they are macabre and bestial, sometimes they are caused by mere loss of temper. The florentine police hardly ever leave such undetected. They are less successful, as all police forces are, with casual crimes like smash-and-grab, bag-snatching and the pilfering of

---

[1] Rumbustious, hasty-tempered, wild sculptor and goldsmith of the later Renaissance. Not all the claims to technical achievement and immorality made in his autobiography, however, are necessarily true.

luxury cameras from luxury cars left ostentatiously at kerbs. Though even with these they often get astonishing results within a few hours.

Nor do I mean the *malavita*, the underworld of drugs, perversions, gangsterdom, which every now and then throws up a shocking delict and centres in the Cascíne, where it is unwise to go alone after dark.

Nor misdemeanours either, like 'pappagallism' (= Parrotry, a word applied to youths who molest girls in public places). These are galling to lady visitors. Young men shadow, follow and sometimes assault pretty girls: a regrettable survival from times when only prostitutes walked alone. But sometimes this is the unconscious fault of the girl. The British Consulate was once invaded by a band of kilted, hairy-kneed and indignant young Scots demanding a glencoe revenge on a lady's hairdresser who had made advances to a customer, their friend. It appeared that the hairdresser had misinterpreted the gay, free glances of the young lassie, to which he was quite unused, and perhaps her italian too or the signs she made in its stead.

It used to be said that in Scotland girls looked at men as they pleased if an interesting one passed, while in London they only peeped out of the corners of their eyes. In Italy a girl can do neither of these, or she will have a bunch of comment-passing, offer-making youths at her heels for the rest of her walk. There is hardly a man in the whole peninsula who does not feel it a matter of male pride, indeed duty, to make passes at all women everywhere. Whether they all welcome a successful issue, I do not know. But friendly foreign girls, especially open american ones, can get into serious trouble if they behave as at home.[1] Which is why many of them wear sun-glasses even on rainy days.

---

[1] 'I gave him a lift' said a beautiful foreign woman motorist. 'And he offered me a thousand lire to go to bed with him. That's two dollars. I'd have thought I was worth more.'

Florentine girls need use neither sun-glasses nor the corners of their eyes. They do not miss much.

Hooligans too there are. Sometimes they take advantage of Hogmanay, when from every window in the centre of the city, as the bells ring-in the New Year, anything recently broken is flung out on the pavement to be broken more, from cups, jugs, glasses and plates to plaster ornaments and plastic lavatory seats. Any inhabitant who has to be out keeps to the middle of the road, and even that doesn't always save his head. The hooligans, infected by this orgy of crash, take to motorcar wind-screens, newspaper kiosks, madonnas and traffic signs, at that hour undefended.

When the maroon Alvis was still in Fiesole, she was raped one night by such hooligans. They smashed the headlamps, unscrewed and stole the red rear glasses, and even went off with the radiator cap, a simple but beautiful and to them useless chromium disc. The car was grounded till spares could be flown from Coventry. On these I paid customs duty, and was told I could recover it on leaving the country, if I produced the broken parts at the frontier.

When I denounced this contemptible act to the local police, the sergeant let out a cry. 'But nobody in Fiesole would do such a thing! They come up from Florence. We'll never find them.' They never did.

Crimes and misdemeanours happen in all cities: it is not in this sense that I call the Florentines incurable law-breakers, but in relation to the law in general, and all of them.

The view of the police is that all civilians, being the law-breakers they undoubtedly are, must be kept under strict control. And there are at least five kinds of police: the Carabineri (very smart when in dress uniform on sundays), the City Police[1] (with their mobile squads), the Traffic Police (with theirs), the Railway Police, and the Financial Police

[1] Civilian reports of thefts often get lost between Carabinieri and City Police, each saying it's the other's concern.

(who jail you for life if you grow a leaf of tobacco). There may be other breeds not listed at Crufts.[1]

All of these order people about like the militia of Moscow, and often as curtly. On point duty there are always two: one to wave his arms and blow his whistle, the other to fine on the spot any driver or pedestrian who has offended. Florentine officers on point duty are less flamboyant than roman ones, whose elegant, accurate, continuous gestures would have done credit to Sir Thomas Beecham. The Florentines have sterner eyes, minimum gestures, and sometimes apoplectic flushes of blood to the forehead. If it rains too hard, they stand in doorways and study traffic problems.

But it is also the law that makes the lawlessness.

The central government seems to think that all Italians are sicilian bandits, criminals, degenerates and cheats, or would be if not controlled. It is true that even traffic problems can lead to crime. Not long ago a milanese professional man was so displeased at being overtaken when driving up to some traffic lights, that he took out a revolver and shot the offender (whom he did not know) dead.[2] But this is a neurotic exception. In general, Italians are just as capable of good driving as any other nation. Indeed many Florentines have expressed to me their envy of british road habits, where very little bad driving is anything more than bad manners. In Italy almost every mistake is a contravention, liable to a fine. In consequence, there can be no question of good manners, which are as much self-esteem as social sense. In Italy self-esteem makes a driver break as many rules as he can get away with. This, I hope, has been taken into consideration by those in Britain who advocate a codification of driving offences.

Offences, contraventions, here are many. (Perhaps not so many, however, as the collateral charges which can be brought

[1] For example there is a branch called the *Polizia Annona* which seems to have something to do with the distribution of food. The *Squadra del Buon Costume*'s duties are to go about arresting prostitutes, and even, if they choose, couples who embrace in public. See p. 220.   [2] This, however, was in Milan.

against a british motorist who dents his mudguard on a tree.[1])
Here it is useless to argue or protest. It is equally useless to
apologise, which may be taken as cover for some worse
offence. It is dangerous to counterattack. Many an honest
citizen or visitor has been sentenced to jail for fifteen days
by immediate summary trial for telling a policeman he was
discourteous.

It is true these are immediately released to provisional
liberty: but this depends on their keeping their temper during
proceedings. It is not a very democratic system. But of course
anyone foolish enough to allude to fascism in a policeman's
presence will not get his provisional liberty. This leads to a lot
of hypocrisy.

It is best to pay the fine of 11s 6d as soon as possible and say
nothing. Whoever stays long enough in Florence is bound to
come up against the police sooner or later. He is safer if he
behaves like a Florentine.

This is not to say that the police exploit foreign visitors. On
the contrary, I have tried to pay a parking offence fine and
had my ticket torn up at the pay-office as not being meant for
tourists.

Nor is it to say that they cannot be courteous, helpful and
kind, if treated reasonably. Many have a sense of humour.
An old lady was crossing where four roads meet, in the days
when trafficlights were manipulated by a kind of push-button
held in a policeman's hand and connected to a wall control-
box. She took no notice of the red light, but crossed diagonally,
so that cars shot at her from several directions. The policeman
blew his whistle. The old lady lost her nerve, stepping this
way and that, first forward, then back, then sideways.
'Madam!' called the policeman in broad florentine, instead of
arresting her, 'Have the courage of your convictions!'

There is a school on the outskirts of the town, where one of

---

[1] I have been threatened in Glasgow with a fine of two pounds for leaving the rear
wheels of a car overlapping by a foot or so a white line in a parking place.

Italy's main routes divides in two, and the trolleybuses stop. A father taking his children to school each morning foresaw serious accidents if the little cars hurtling down to business were not controlled. At that hour some came through the village, others from the open country. None ever took notice of the pedestrian crossing nor even slowed up despite speed limit and traffic signs.

Meeting a policeman in a local café this father asked if someone could not stand with a warning notice-board of 'Children Crossing,' as old age pensioners do in Britain and some other countries. The policeman was decidedly against. Such a civilian would be obstructing the traffic, a contravention for any but the police, who must keep this privilege. If anything went wrong, it would be the civilian's fault, not the driver's. 'But' he added 'if you wish to make a *denuncia*, the *Questore* will consider it.'[1]

To make a *denuncia*, or indeed any application to any official of any kind, you must buy at the tobacconist's a piece of special foolscap costing about 4s 4d, and begin it 'The Undersigned John Doe or Richard Roe, candle-maker, resident at No. 335 Park Street and domiciled at No. 51 (red) Teddyboy Square . . .' or it will never get read. There is even a special lay-out, with a large left-hand margin, which I am sure makes more than one bored civil servant look at the contents.

'O no!' said the father, whose social sense was somewhat developed, 'The police have other things to do than stand outside every school in Florence.'

So he did nothing. But the following week there was a policeman holding up the little cars for the children to cross both going into school and coming out, and there has been one almost every day ever since.

So necessities do sometimes penetrate by mere word through the papier-maché walls of offices.

---

[1] The *Questore* is, roughly, the Chief Constable.

There is one other symptom of locality that must be mentioned here. Just as in other countries with some past culture one can see men and women today with faces of the type that peer down from eighteenth and seventeenth century portraits, so in Florence one sees faces of the florentine Renaissance. It is not easy to spot in the street a 'florentine type.' Black eyes, raven hair, the sallow neapolitan features which are in Britain often called 'italian,' these are not to be seen, or belong to incomers from the south. Grey eyes, blue eyes, green eyes, hazel eyes, brown eyes whether pure brown or varying into other dark hues, these Yes: and brown hair, fair hair, golden hair, sometimes red hair, and not impossibly flaxen hair in very young children: for Florentines are as much a mixture of the north and the mediterranean as the people of Glasgow are mixed Celts and Saxons. But time and time again in the street one carries with one the flash of an image of a face by Giotto, or the wistful eyes and sensitive cheekbones of a Botticelli. These are not italian but florentine. They will appear again later.

In the meantime let us hear what Florentines think about themselves.

8

Florentines on Florentines

Piazza Santa Croce was once a swamp, dotted with miserable huts, place of folk even humbler than the Thin Folk who succeeded them. Then orchards and craftsmen's shops came there, and in due course among them was opened up this long wide space with the great church at one end and a palazzo or two on the sides.

This was the true people's space in the city. In the fourteenth century the people clustered to hear the preachings of franciscan friars who had no church. In the fifteenth, they came to see the jousts and tourneys of young nobles. Lorenzo de' Medici was victor here in 1468. In the sixteenth century the people gathered to watch the Football Game, a rough and bloody business with no holds barred, so dear to them that in 1529, during the Siege, defiant music was played from the roof of the church to drown the enemy guns.

Now it is full of parked cars, resting long-distance touring coaches and a hideous statue of Dante, which is shortly to be removed, so that the football game can return to its original quarters.

The houses round the Piazza are constructed like those of Edinburgh: a common entrance door, a common stair. At the top sometimes there is an extra staircase leading to an attic, which has a small balcony overlooking the square, sweet and cool after summer heat.

On one of these balconies two florentine ladies were sipping iced vodka and tomato juice and looking out on the fresco-decorated façade, pallid in reflected light, of a sixteenth century palazzo. They were discussing a third florentine lady, Eugenia, who was not present.

Eugenia some time before had gone all out to grab the man she wanted licitly or illicitly. She had made no secret of this. Everybody knew.

But her man threw her off.

'I hardly know her now' said Donatella, 'She was radiant. Now she's gone bitter. Like a witch.'

'She felt the humiliation' said Giulia. 'It was all so public.'

Donatella sipped. 'That needn't make one bitter. Not all the time, about everything.'

Her friend leaned forward. 'Listen' she said 'Never forget that we are Florentines, all of us, bankers and merchants still, at heart. We can go bankrupt once, but never again.'

'*Già*' Donatella agreed. '*Giusto!*'

9

To Touch a Donatello

As in Tuscany almost every hill is crowned with a villa, a small town, a castle, a monastery or a farmstead, with the result that the whole countryside whether fertile or not seems man-made and functional; so round Florence every hill and rise is coronetted with villas, a crowd of family life. No matter how crooked the approach nor in what ganglion of cottages these lie, they all have views over the city.

The villas of the prosperous have depended on the agile fingers in the small shops since at least the end of the sixteenth century, when Ariosto described them as 'buds' on the hills. Florence to him looked like two Romes, poised on the sides of the valley which had become entirely her property as far down as the sea at Pisa and Livorno, through a plain that is now filling up with factories and modern houses among smallholdings of tomatoes, maize, peaches and artichokes. And little villages too, which for centuries have depended not only on the ungenerous soil but also on the fingers of those who weave articles out of straw.[1]

The villas are of every type, large or small, ancient or modern, formal or homely, but they fall into two main categories. There are those, mainly of the fifteenth to eighteenth centuries with enclosed gardens and high walls: and there are those whose gardens slide out without a frontier into the

[1] Leghorn hats, for example, which were the rage among victorian ladies, were exported from Leghorn (Livorno) but made in the valley of the Arno. Straw hats are still worn by tuscan contadini, many of whom would not dream of working in the hot sun without one.

countryside, so that a guest walks from a cluster of jasmin round a garden door through flowerbeds into cauliflowers and so into a cornfield. Roses bloom between olive trees and even, I regret to say, sometimes up them.

Some have frescoes of the seventeenth and eighteenth centuries. Some have private chapels, now used as outhouses or not used at all. Round some there still hangs an odour of farmyard byres or olive presses or new wine. One near San Domenico had an open-air theatre where plays and musical shows were given. In the last century one had a private theatre that seated 800. And each has its own character, is an architectural individual, not like any other.

Some are family residences still occupied by the titled descendants of the men who built them. But the ownership of most has passed to later rich men and women, including foreigners, or for use as schools and institutions. The Villa Schifanoia is run for foreign girls as a kind of research or finishing centre by gay nuns. One at Bellosguardo, very famous, shelters mainly american girl students, who are delivered down into Florence in a small bus like pullets going to market and can have as teacher of italian literature so un-academic a person as Alberto Moravia.[1] Another has recently been taken over by a famous typewriter firm as a warehouse and college for typewriters. After cramped quarters in a narrow street in the centre, the staff now breathes good air and can park its cars in the garden.

The older villas tend to be very formal. Michelozzo's great summer palace for the Medici family under Fiesole costs a million lire a year to heat inadequately; and the interior has been much altered since the days when Donatello and Pico della Mirandola came to supper with Lorenzo de' Medici. Nor are its vast chambers easy to make comfortable. But it was found convenient some years ago by a french consul, because

---

[1] Novelist of the present day, several of whose novels have been translated into english: e.g. *The Woman of Rome*.

it gave him room for the archaeological collection he had made in the Middle East.

Formal gardens can be oppressive to british and american people. It is fine to see outside your windows fields of daffodils and tall trees golden with mimosa balls; but a geometrical projection of cypresses at a marble temple or herm can humiliate present occupiers as they take a turn in the garden before breakfast, unless they have antecedents whom they can imagine having done likewise.

In the last century, when the British were the majority among permanent foreign residents, they liked to reproduce the atmosphere of gardens known in Britain. Hence one can still find in bloom old-fashioned roses on trunks as thick as old vine stems, which have quite deserted the catalogues and are to be found nowhere else, except perhaps in Germany or Holland. The results are not always show-places, but have charm and surprise.

I know an american lady who grows very tall and perfumed sweet peas which flower in march, whereas sweet peas are generally poor, by comparison, in Florence. She has also a very tall bay-tree, the leaves of which used to be bought and stripped before the last war by german merchants for potting herring. And some of the trees are astonishing: gigantic cedars of Lebanon: the biggest holm-oak in Tuscany.

But it is more with the contents of the villas that this chapter is concerned.

Among a group of modern suburban houses stands a thirteenth century tower with frescoes of that period on its walls. But also on the walls hang what look like framed pictures with roll-up curtains over them. They are not pictures but musical manuscripts: Beethoven, Bach, Mozart, name whom you like. The most unexpected, and most in need of its little blind to keep off the sun, is a song by Mendelssohn at the head of which the composer himself painted a romantic water-colour.

There is another villa which Botticelli used to visit. It contains a head believed to be by Donatello. Another contains unique musical instruments used by at least three world-famous players. And I do not mention renaissance masterpieces in the homes of professional collectors.

There is one with a Botticelli so early that it is practically mediaeval gilding. There are works by Michelangelo in another, said to be uncatalogued. The proprietor of a third has an untouched etruscan tomb in his garden, kept secret because of a national law that makes all such discoveries the property of Rome. A Professor of Etruscology, to inspect it, had to dress up as an electrician's assistant.

The most surprising possession of all is in a house not at all ancient.

This house was built by an American who came to Florence for a fortnight and stayed over fifty years. (Florence does this to many, but few reach these figures.) He designed it himself. By florentine standards it is not a big house, by London ones it is distinctly Upper Ten. Nor is it an imitation. It has no lofty ceilings, no huge spiky dangling ironwork lanterns. It has large windows. It is full of light and air and life and even that unfashionable quality, joy.

In the garden (which is that of the sweet peas and the bay tree) stands an enormous roman-empire fountain bowl of porphyry, one of very few in the world, which this American picked up in Naples in fragments. It is now so watertight that it has to be protected in winter, in case frost should crack it by the rain it holds.

Inside the house are other classical things, among them a statuette fascinatingly poised between roman and greek. The extremities and the thick toga are roman, but the feel of the cloth at the back pure greek, the flesh palpable through diaphanous folds on shoulder and buttock.

Inside the door is a good Bronzino portrait, which makes you pause. But when you enter the sitting room you stop dead.

On each side of the fireplace is a lifesize wooden statue. St John the Baptist is on your right; the one on the left is said to be St John the Divine, but this could be disputed, seeing that he holds in his left hand not a book but what seems to be the base of a broken chalice. He may be by Verrocchio. The Baptist is definitely by Donatello, as the feet alone would tell. He makes occasional trips to exhibitions.

Wisely, the walls of this room, pleasantly proportioned, are quite bare. There is nothing on them at all. There are no pictures in the room; but on the furniture, the grand piano, everywhere are vases of garden flowers, lavish, multicoloured.

A fullsize Donatello in the family is a thing I have never come across before. One has to contrast it with the paraded figures in the Bargello, with the untouchable remoteness of the saints of Orsanmichele or the choir stalls in the Duomo Museum. Even with the warmth of the Santa Croce Annunciation, for that is untouchable too.

But this is touchable. And the touch is revelation.

The hand of the other saint, a softer figure, has the feel of the wood it is made of. The hand of the Baptist seems to pulse with blood. It feels like a human hand, not wood at all. Put palm to palm, and it seems about to interlace fingers or fold yours into a fist. A gentle, friendly hand. The hand of a saint.

We arrived in Florence without introductions, and knowing nobody.

IO ❧

L' Impruneta[1]

The crowd moved slow as cattle, congealing round the cars that crept up the sun-baked lane. Many engines, not powerful enough to go slow, stalled. The walkers behind grazed their shins on the bumperbars. Some drivers risked a breakaway up farm tracks, where metal and mankind clogged again till policemen on red motorbicycles chased them back to the lane like strayed pigs.

In the outskirts of the small town more policemen kept dogs and children off the approach roads. But knowing there would be at least another hour to wait, people who had lined them broke ranks, left their positions and went calling on one another.

An expectant hush settled on the remaining crowd, and shouting policemen headed newcomers off the cleared road.

Another expectant hush settled on the remaining crowd and shouting policemen headed more newcomers off the cleared road.

Music was heard from the left. It mingled with music from the right. Two bands appeared.

Each band was led by groups of young men in *cinquecento* costume, elegant, rich-coloured, magnificent, teams of the ancient Football Game of Florence on parade. Their proud profiles by-passed centuries: Andrea del Sarto portraits trod the road. The sun leaped on pikes, helmets, halberds. The hot air flowed with music.

[1] L'Impruneta is a small town near and to the South-east of Florence. The church contains a Madonna which several times in the past has been solemnly carried through florentine streets to maintain morale in moments of communal danger.

Then came carts, rolling forward behind pairs or foursomes of white oxen, low carts surmounted by sculpture in bunches of grapes. Each, summoned by heralds, paused for a while in front of the judges and important people at the upper side of the sloping Piazza. They used brakes.

First, a great bell, six-feet-high, made entirely of purple bunches slung on a timber frame upholstered with vine leaves. In the bow of that cart sat a black-haired beauty in red satin with yellow and black sleeves. With a rope of twined vine-stems she tolled a clapper of green grape bunches. In the stern sat a blonde beauty in white and primrose-leaf green and gold, like the coming of spring. With lazy grace and a pert pout she tossed down bunches of grapes to the up-stretching crowd.

Her heavy-lidded eyes were pure Piero della Francesca.

Next, a smaller cart carried accurate models of florentine buildings, the Duomo, the Signoría, San Lorenzo, Giotto's Tower, all of grapes crammed close as a mulberry. It carried also a banner with the name of the area of vineyards which had constructed it, as each cart did.

Then a huge float long as a viking ship with a scene of the harvest called THIS YEAR. Round a central cabin, redolent of autumn, sat a whole busied family: a young son playing an accordion while his bride sang; the old mother shouting jests at the crowds, and grandchildren, polished like stones, their eyes like jewels, flung bunches over a living hedge. THF FOUR SEASONS followed, each a beautiful girl coming out of a winepress like buckets on a dredger. Blondes and brunettes stripped off vivid mantles and stood in vivider limbs.

EX VITE VITA read the next title: Out of the Vine, Life! An inn, colourful couples dancing in the doorway, a big glass tumbler on the roof supported by vats brimming with grape. Beautifully timed to this appearance on the piazza and to the drift of the breeze overhead, a small biplane, circling and crossing, released leaflets of pastel-pink and green and blue, which fluttered and tumbled like wings without birds in the bright sun, soared over housetops, were clutched-in at windows and scrambled-for on the ground. On these were printed the words of the song now being sung on the float, a hymn in rough verse to the bloodred ray of the sun imprisoned in the grape.

Astride an upturned vat, unsteadily wobbling as couples danced round her, a film starlet drained a silver goblet. This was BEAUTY. A muscular man and a youth raised and lowered seemingly heavy weights. This was STRENGTH. A small boy climbed a ladder up a gothic castle to embrace a gold-tressed maiden (of his own size) in a window (or should I say casement?), while an old woman, spinning below, expressed romantic disapproval. This was LOVE. And the whole was INVENTIVENESS (*Fantasía*) without which Man cannot live.

It would have done credit to a Triumph at the medicean court.

This crowd had not been demonstrative. Applause was rare: it cheered not at all. It waited for the evening, when wine would flow. It had a few handclaps for the kisses blown by the starlet. For centuries the Florentines have been called 'sober' by poets and others.

But when the trumpet blew, the crowd tensed. In front of the judges now stood a huge haystack on wheels. The trumpet, winding, rising, falling, took the highest note.

At that there was a very loud bang. The top of the haystack blew open like a paper bag, and a flight of pigeons flapped skyward almost as perpendicular as ants going up a tree. In the same rhythm of wing they reached the same level, wheeled horizontally, and settled on cornices round the rhomboid piazza, shaking their feathers.

A real shout of joy went up, with a hurricane of applause that made the pigeons leap in the air again and settle again. And almost at once the multitude started to dissolve, like the motion of vine leaves in a sudden breeze. Adjoining streets roared into an activity of motors, motorbikes and motor-scooters. The afternoon was over.

The sun weakened. The sky paled. In the entrance to the Piazza coloured lights came on. They glittered and poured red wine, or formed bright vine-leaves half-floating on a rigid wind.

The Feast began.

Going to School

There are two kinds of schools in Italy, state and private. The state schools, administered from Rome, are divided into primary, middle, and then gymnasiums and lyceums. The lyceums are specialised, in arts, classics, science, mechanics, because by the time the pupils get there they are supposed to know their own bents. Owing to lack of space lyceums and gymnasiums are often in the same buildings. Inside this specialisation if the pupil qualifies, he or she can then go on to any university in Italy they choose.

Age can bring surprises. Although one knows that italian girls mature earlier than british ones, it is always a shock to see female forms ripe for Girton or Somerville popping in and out of dayschools with schoolboys. Age however is all important to Rome. If your child is six years old on the 31st of december, he can go to school in his proper year. If born on the 1st of january, he stays out for twelve months.

The remote and paper control of roman bureaucrats brings nonsensical hardship on teachers. One who was wife and mother in Florence suddenly found herself a permanent grass widow in Trieste. An unmarried cousin of ours with family ties in Rome had to make a daily double journey south of Naples. It is true the state railways give teachers reductions on fares: but so they do to a high proportion of italian citizens, because a high proportion of italian citizens is state employed. This does not much help the teachers.

Any child that qualifies can attend any school. Since some schools have a better reputation than others, parents spend part of their mornings and afternoons chauffeuring their children across the city. Reputation, however, by no means always leads to healthy competition, because headmasters being state employees draw their salaries whether the public likes their work or not, and it is as heinous an offence to insult a headmaster as it is to insult a policeman or any other public officer.

Nevertheless, thanks to the teachers, most of whom are as dedicated to their craft as those in Britain, the standard is high and sound, fully as high and sound as ours, if perhaps to our taste the pace is somewhat forced. Many teachers take a deep personal interest in their children, and in the primary schools move up with them class by class.

There are a few private schools called colleges, where the pupils live-in. These are nothing like english public schools, partly because the pupils include well-to-do children who cannot make the grade in state schools and difficult children who have no wish to.

Nuns run a large number of private schools. Their standards vary, except that of their will to educate and care for. Their pupils range from kindergarten to university age and sit the state examinations. But despite the Concordat between Mussolini and the Vatican,[1] which the present form of italian democracy confirmed, the state contributes nothing to this adjunct of its service. The nuns have to depend on such fees as parents can pay or such charity as the nuns can wheedle.

In state schools religious instruction is given by the local priest, since it is he who has to prepare children for First Communion; also for Confirmation, which, if the Bishop is busy, may surprisingly follow, instead of being a qualification for, First Communion. First Communion for little girls is picturesque. Even the poorest dress like white brides and most become for a while rather pious round this their second (and

---

[1] Italy ceased to be a catholic country in 1803 and did not become one again till the creation of the Vatican City in 1929.

first conscious) public festivity on the road from Baptism to Coming Out (if in that income group), to Betrothal, Marriage, and Death.

But because of difficulties in practising contraception, or maybe reluctance to do it, there are many illegitimate children, and in Florence as in other cities orphans and orphanages abound. These too are run by groups of nuns, large or small.

One is the magnificent Ospedale degli Innocenti, Brunelleschi's masterpiece of architecture, with Andrea della Robbia's swaddled babies studding the architrave on their blue discs. This was actually founded on the public Hospital of San Gallo which Florence started in the twelfth century. Its present form and fame are due to the Art of the Silk Workers in 1419. The people of Florence called it after the Massacre of the Innocents by Herod, a fate from which it has saved uncountable young lives in 700 years, most of whom were given 'degli Innocenti' as a surname: so that today the telephone directory contains four columns of degli Innocenti heads of families and six columns without the definite article. But now such orphans are given other surnames.

On the other hand orphan schools can be run by as few as seven nuns. You find them in old buildings in drab streets or in bright new premises with gardens. Some of these orphanages have priceless frescoes on their walls, which have been theirs for generations; some have serene cloisters. Others make do. But in the atmosphere of all, or very, very nearly all, there is peace and love and compassion in its proper sense, founded not on dogma but on fact and a sense of human values.

Many of the children are not foundlings without known parents. Their parents are known. They have been abandoned because the parents parted or both for work went to different cities.

So on the outskirts little nuns[1] may be seen driving little buses every day into town to collect their pupils from family

---

[1] Has anyone ever explained why nuns are nearly always little?

homes. The nun of today has no milk-and-water piety. She may know more about psychology than you do. I have seen one driving a big american car (and priests on motor scooters are a common sight): but that was in Rome near the Segretariato. She was physically beautiful as many nuns are. All have a professional attitude to their jobs.

Therefore if you are drinking vermouth or lemonade in a café and a couple of nuns hold out their hands, or if you go to the Central Post Office and notice two sitting and waiting in a corner near the main door, pause before you decide not to give a coin or two. They may be collecting for some such institution as I have told of, which has no subsidies whatever, sparse grants from other houses in its Order, small help if any from the Church: and school fees rarely cover a new cooker, certainly not an efficient heating system.

Your gift will be better spent than on the permanent beggar woman with baby who touches rich strangers in the Via Tornabuoni or on the gipsies who invade Florence from time to time with their lovely clear-eyed children. You may not get a word of thanks from them, still less a blessing. For some have an abstracted look, as if their thoughts were elsewhere, as if they had no business with the sordid gathering of coins, as indeed they should not need to have. As indeed is the truth.

The fresh, clean, neat, eager side of italian education is thus partly provided by nuns. In this, however, we must also include kindergartens, which are provided by local government (*Comune*). To judge by our own experience, the standard of these is very high, for ours is not one of specially great repute, but a modest, ordinary one in a hamlet on the outskirts. Apart from the first day of a first term, when there is sure to be some small boy or girl in tears at having to face for four hours unknown society instead of known home, its members go to it as to a Small Persons' Club. Every moment and movement is interesting or exciting in a world of development. In their play they begin to learn, under a young teacher-mother devoted and brilliant. At the end of each term they bring home toys and gifts they have made for their parents with paper and glue, or calendars at New Year. They learn to sing songs, old patriotic famous ones, little folk songs, slightly sugary religious ones, even Alpini songs,[1] which make a bond of common culture out of school hours. They have, provided free, all kinds of playthings large and small which are also educational, mentally or physically. They learn to make pictures, and hold exhibitions. Sometimes there is a puppet show.

At kindergarten as at school children work in the mornings only, saturdays included: but they can go back in the afternoons, the school children to do their 'prep' (*doposcuola*) or to have extra-curriculum lessons in french or english at the primary school. As only an hour passes between morning and afternoon, a cook comes to prepare lunch for such as stay. Until a year ago this meal was free, and all that a parent paid for a year's schooling was the 800 lire for registration, about 10s. But with the rise in the cost of living, even more severe in Italy than in Britain for non-luxuries, a charge had to be made, and lunch now costs 1s 9d. At this meal the grocer's son eats with the daughter of a well-to-do fashion designer, with the offspring of the local drunkard, and with the child of a Count, if it suits the parents to leave them there that day. This does good to all.

Summer holidays are much longer than ours in Britain—from the middle of june to the end of september. Christmas and Easter holidays are much shorter—only a few days. But Holy Week is not observed so strictly in Italy as it is in Episcopal England: nor by the public in general. Good Friday is not a holiday; and shops and offices stay open on the Saturday as on all saturdays. On the other hand Easter Monday, being the Feast of the Angel, is a public holiday as in Britain, and Florence makes for the mountains or the sea.

However, nobody is allowed to know the exact date when

[1] See chapter 18.

any school term begins or ends until the bureaucrats in Rome have decided on it—which usually they do not do till a day or two before.

School books are bought in ordinary scholastic bookshops, of which there are few in Florence. What books are to be studied is announced, like the opening date, only a day or two before: with the result that a parent must spend two to three hours in queues, where hundreds of them if they have contrived to spare time off work or cannot find anyone to mind their children, stand, wait, push and scrum in dumb riot.

Exercise books, on the other hand, with their appropriate lines or squares, are found in local bars. The commercial interest of the USA is not seen at its best in Italy. Not only do shops have to sell products of the lowest quality consistent with the law, such as brushless shaving soaps that do not lather, bicarbonate of soda that does not dissolve in water, and biscuits that are just edible; but also patriotic US propaganda is directed at italian schoolchildren, on the jesuit or communist principle of catching them young. Thus the end papers of one of my daughter's copy books illustrate the speed records of the world. Those of land and air are given full credits, being american. Bluebird, being british, is described merely as 'very fast.'

But the USA got into Europe very quickly after the Marshall Plan.

Inside school terms there are several free days: some for church festivals like Corpus Domini and All Saints, others for certain of the national holidays commemorating historical changes. But Italy is not like the Spain I used to know, where almost every other day could be a holiday, especially in winter—excellent excuses for avoiding difficult interviews.

Other free days are less predictable. One morning the janitors of all schools will strike, being state employees: another, those of kindergartens, being employed by the local government. Teachers can strike under orders from their union. But then almost everybody in Italy strikes. Either for an hour or two like bus drivers at peak hours: or for days like dockers and railwaymen. Sometimes together, as when country busmen join city busmen; sometimes alone as taxi-drivers. Doctors and dentists strike, even hospital doctors. Hospital staffs strike. Magistrates strike.

Even the police, recently, went on strike. But this was a serious matter, and the government talks of an enquiry into this desertion of duty to their service. Duty to their service, be it understood, not in regard to the public, but to the state. The armed forces, of which the police are part, are not considered as a service to the public.

The only people who cannot strike are ordinary citizens without Unions, or whose unions do not regard their complaints as important. Try to organise a strike among parents because a school is being badly run, or a procession of householders on foot across a dangerous and neglected road, and you will find that the state has a law to land you with, and jail or fines to follow.

Indifference, irritation and tyranny from Rome do not stop at the school. They affect also children's health. If a child has had a rusty hook taken out of its heel in a state children's hospital (all hospitals are state hospitals) it cannot have anti-tetanus vaccine injected there at once, but must be taken to a chemist's to buy it. The chemist cannot give the injection: nobody but a doctor may. Neither can a a doctor in a state hospital for adults. Only the one children's hospital in Florence. And by the time the child gets back there it has lost its place in the queue.

If a child is away from school for a day, he or she must bring next morning a note from a parent explaining the cause, more or less truthfully. This is fair enough. A birthday can be 'family business.' A daytrip to the country can be covered by a fictitious headache or slight temperature. These are accepted locally with tact and understanding.

But if a child is away for five days, even from lack of transport, the state closes in. Loyal to its miles of conserved forms and reports, doubtless, Rome insists on the child being taken to a control centre for medical investigation. Here the victims wait in a queue all morning (there are few such centres, and these being state offices are open only in the mornings). The inspecting doctor (when he arrives) will issue a certificate that the child shows no signs of having been exposed to an infectious disease (a negative which does not mean much), such as the child after five days in the fresh air alone with its parents may well have in fact picked up while waiting in the old-fashioned, ill-ventilated office crammed with waiting children.

The reason for this extraordinary manifestation of bureaucracy is that italian lawmakers will not believe in the integrity of the family doctor. They are convinced that he will endanger his professional reputation for a shilling or two or out of sheer kindness. 'How wouldn't he?' mutters the Law. 'He is only a citizen like the rest: sheep or wolf.'

But the citizens of Florence are not wolves, even if the Law does make them break the Law. If they may seem like sheep, it is a kind of sheep hitherto unknown. In relation to shepherds and their dogs they may go whither they are driven, as they have been forced to do for centuries of mutton. But in their minds they reserve judgment, and their minds are very active. Within the limits of the imposed Law they have a sense of justice not unlike that of the Cockney's ' 'Taint right, somehow': at which point, if it is reached, it is no use the Law telling the Cockney to do, or not to do, anything, as London lawmakers know.

The Florentines accept what comes, as the older Scots accepted the Will of the Lord. They withdraw into themselves for freedom. A dangerous situation, as we will be seeing. But sheep panic when chased. Florentines, as also we will be seeing, do not. And their children grow like them.

12

Concerning Forest Fires

It was at the height of a dry summer. Above a by-pass skirting a small village inside the confines of Florence there was a clump or colony of post-Lloyd-Wright houses, more glass than local stone or concrete, angular, buoyant, filled with light, fitting their owners like well-tailored suits. These had been first drawn on paper by an architect famous in Italy and America, and then, as most italian houses are, realised and constructed by building engineers.

In them lived a number of artists, at least one of them being world-famous. The inhabitants not only looked out on an eye-arresting view: the view came through their absence of blockage and sat on their furniture. It was part of their personal minutes.

In the early hours of one morning a lorry rolled down the by-pass below. The world-famous painter was sleepless and watched it from her window. Out of the cabin a red cigarette-end flew into the trees and brushwood that covered the up-ward slope. Within an hour the whole copse was ablaze, fanning up to the houses above. The residents came out in dressing-gowns. Some ran their cars out to safety. Some took sticks and brooms and went down to fight the flames: yellow brooms, fan-shaped, the mediaeval kind seen in pictures of witches, which are the best for uncarpeted floors of polished brick or travertine.

Fortunately the painter had a big reserve of water in her household tank, and her husband sprayed the nearest area of ground with his garden hose.

Much later, when the fire brigade arrived, it deliberated with itself how to put out a fire. It also had a tank, but its hoses reached only halfway up the slope, and the garden hose only a quarter down. It was decided to put out the fire by leaving it alone, as it was isolated by water. In due time it died down, and the residents went back to bed in woodsmoke.

Not long after, there was another fire, this time by daylight, probably started the same way, higher up the by-pass, where it makes a big curve to rejoin the old road. A knoll on the lower side was fully ablaze. Flames had crept down a dell and up a brae, so that they threatened traffic on the curve. There was a good stiff breeze, and sparks or burning twiglets of pine and other resinous trees floated over the roadway, likely to arrive in the wooded slope on the higher side, and so spread along to the colony of new houses.

One of the artists, a foreigner, who had come out to see, decided to organise a little fire-fighting. He took two household brooms, one new, one old, and went over the parapet in his sandals. Before long a dozen cars had stopped, and drivers and passengers got out to look. He called to them to come down and help, but nobody moved. He went on beating.

He went round to attack from below. The hard ground quickly released burning turves and bits of blazing wood down on him. His feet were singed by smoulderers slowly gnawing. Pausing to rest, he saw that the bodies on the parapet above had increased in number. There were now some uniforms. The fire brigade also was looking on.

Indignant, sweating, grimy, sore and out of breath, he scrambled up and asked the officer in charge if they couldn't help.

'We've no water' was the reply. Indeed the fire float had no tank.

'Well' said the foreigner, 'let's get those people along there to work with sticks and brooms. There must be forty of them.'

'And where are the brooms?' asked the officer in friendly

florentine humour. No brooms are supplied in areas liable to
fire.

'There are sticks' retorted the foreigner. 'And your men at
least can help.'

'I would willingly give you a hand myself' the officer
observed 'but today I have put on my new uniform.'

Nobody moved.

'It isn't' said a fireman 'as though there were houses in
danger. By the Law we protect only houses. Here there is
nothing but trees.'

('The Law' is the word used by all officials and civil servants
to describe their instructions and directives.)

'Nothing but trees!' muttered the foreigner and plunged
down to tackle a new outbreak.

When he was sure he had done all he could, he came up to
the road again, and found nobody there but a man on a
motor-bicycle waiting for him.

'Was it you that sent for me?' this man demanded severely.

'And who are you?' asked the foreigner.

'I'm the Road Superintendant for this section. Somebody
telephoned for me to come as there was a fire. I see no fire.'

'I put it out.'

'It wasn't threatening the road. You shouldn't have sent for
me.'

'It could have threatened not only the road but those
houses there.'

'I have come twenty-five kilometres for nothing.'

The foreigner lost patience. He described in detail what
might have happened, how it might have happened, and what
he had done to prevent it happening. 'Is it right that this should
be left to one man?'

The Superintendent went ironical. 'Very well' he said,
'you're a hero! We're having a reunion over in Fiesole next
week. I'll take you as my guest and present you as the man
who put out a fire singlehanded!'

He even tried to catch the foreigner's wrist for a mock handshake.

The foreigner went home with two hot black poles which had been brooms, and a rage against bureaucracy equal only to the author's.

'That may be so' said a florentine lawyer later, however, when the foreigner told him. 'But I owe my wood and maybe my house to the Vigili del Fuoco. Twice in a night they came, and worked like blacks. *Brava gente*!'

13

Tale of a Tuscan Garden

This is the tale of a man who knew nothing of gardens and of a garden made in a field of olives.

The field, which contained some olive trees centuries old, was one of several terraced slopes on a hill facing south over Florence. In the middle grew a wild peach, on the edges, three fig trees. It was cut off to the southwest by ilex woods, a few square yards of which were bought with the field.

Ilex woods are indigenous in Tuscany, but a great part of this forest had been of sweet chestnut. The local name for the lane that led to it might best be rendered 'Wee Baas Loan,' 'little balls' being a tuscan phrase for chestnuts. During one of the outbreaks of plague in the fifteenth century many Florentines fled to this spot; but inexorable death followed them, and 'gaean tae the wee baas' still means in Florence 'coming to a sticky end.' This address causes first disbelief, then an embarrassed grin, when the phrase is given in shop or office: all the more because this little known lane lies between Hospital City and the chief cemetery.

The earth between the olives, ploughed each year, had been sown in the previous season with a tall, blue-flowering medick or lucerne. It had stems no hand could pluck and a taproot two feet deep, thick as a snake, which no spade could chop. Each had to be removed with the use of shoulder and loins.

One of the men building the house told him that this fodder crop broke up the soil. The soil needed breaking up. It was made of decomposing flakes of the sandstone of the hill: in summer synthetic rock, in winter malleable mud.

The new owner bought a little book and double-trenched an experimental border by the wood. He sowed giant sunflower and garden balsam, which Italians call 'Handsome Men.' Four or five of the former seeds grew into miniatures an inch or two high; what few of the latter, had no flowers at all. Cosmea and sweet peas stayed dwarf. Pansies were wood violets.

He planted four sickly roots of rhubarb, which is unknown as a dish in Italy. They remained sickly for two years. He planted asparagus, which died of sun and thirst. This mattered less, as there was better and tastier, if less phallic, asparagus growing wild in the wood. He dug celery trenches, because Italians do not bleach their celery: and sowed turnips, because they eat the leaves only and the roots are hard to find in shops. No celery grew, and the turnips came up sparse and woody and small.

By this time the lower end of the experiment was covered with green moss. He wondered if only medick grew near olives.

He bought another little book, and thought again.

By june the roof was on the house, and all repaired to lunch in a trattoría: the family, the architect and wife, the builder and wife, assistants and wives, and all the masons, electricians, carpenters and others working on the house. This is the rule when a new house has its hat on. A flag is stuck on the roof to tell the world.

In the trattoría after the white collars had left, the little feast grew more animated. There is never any thought of going back to work that day: and one of the company grew sun-red in the face and jolly in his speech, with wine.

In the autumn the family moved in to the house. Two of their four black cats died of cat cholera, which sweeps round Florence in biennial cycles. He buried the bodies in the wood and planted snowdrops on the mounds. The snowdrops flowered next year, some stayed the following year, then all disappeared.

Winter came, the second hardest on record. He picked up fallen olives. They rolled into rubble and holes in the ground as numerous as shingle, or played marbles with each other into the field below. His fingers, frozen, could not tell fruit from stone, and neither from the frosted snow they were jewelled in. Snow continued to fall, howling off Alps and Appennines. Three labourers got frostbite. The grocer waded up to the house with provisions. The watermain froze. White snow was boiled for water, and turned black. The grocer waded up with demijohns of drinking water. Without the main, the central heating could not be used. The only fireplace choked in its own smoke. For florentine architects know little of chimney suctions. 'A fireplace' said this one 'is either a birth or an abortion. Yours has aborted.'

In the end the whole family fled to Arezzo where they had cousins in a warm house, as Dante fled to Verona and Macchiavelli to San Casciano, hoping for better times.

When times were better, the gardener bought another two little books and resolved to grow vines, roses and ornamental trees.

He thought himself the possessor of tons of valuable leaf-mould, centuries-rich in the ilex wood. But the wood was dark throughout the year, and suffocated by shrubs of laurustinus with dirty white inflorescences and poisonous-looking purple-black berries. Butcher's broom grew there, red-berried, prickly, which Italians call 'prickmouse' and use as holly at Christmas. There was a cypress or two, a couple of scots pines where squirrels lived, and sessile oaks, their bark lichen-disguised as birch, ghostly pale in the dusk, whose copper leaves stuck on the branches into march. But little else grew. Not hellebore, nor foxgloves, nor even the wild cyclamens which grew well in other parts of the wood. Even a hedgehog, which had delightedly nosed about and galloped round the living room and shared a saucer of milk with the kittens the evening the children caught it, would not stay there. The ground looked, smelt, felt, and was, sour.

He planted a short hedge of *pyracantha yunnanensis* because there had been a splendid specimen of this in his father's garden. It was to be one of the best sights of his own. To protect it from the north wind which was still blowing in february he raised a curtain wall of bricks: and the wind blew the wall down onto one of the young plants so that it always stayed shorter than the others.

He got a labourer to build a retaining fence of posts and boughs along the bank below the garden, because he could not afford to mend the broken retaining wall. Then six lorry-loads of sandy soil from near the Arno came, and another of good mould, which he mixed and barrowed under a sweltering sun, to fill-in the space between fence and bank where the vines would be, and also to make borders along the house and beds beyond it.

He planted eighteen vines, to fruit early, middling and late. First he dug holes in his new mixture, into which he threw bone-manure as a long-term stimulant and added good cow-manure from the two white cattle of a neighbouring farmer. He set his vines, some of which were of french extraction and some of italian; and all, dry sticks like dead twigs with a few root hairs waving in the air. Anyone would have thrown them on the rubbish heap.

He set them in a line more or less straight, and raised over them a gimcrack file of posts and wires to tie the shoots to, if they ever came. These soon drooped and sagged and swayed in the wind, breaking off several shoots, which are fragile especially where they leave the stems. The whole contraption was largely held together in summer by the vines' own tendrils, which despite romantic, modern and even ultra-modern poets are among the toughest things of their kind apart from a two-millimetre steel wire. Try to uncoil them

if they take the wrong place, and you can break your finger-
nails.

But the sight of your first vinebud on your own first vine
is like the feel of your first-born child in your arms for the
first time. You cannot hold the bud. You squat and marvel.

The second year, to his surprise, two vines bore a few grapes.
This was greater reason for marvelling.

When friends call, with a patriarchal feeling one steps into
the garden with a tray or basket, and returns with as many
different bunches, red, pink, or golden, hot from the sun, as is
consistent with being neither ostentatious nor hubristic.

He was not hubristic. Four vines died the first year, possibly
because of their positions. He replaced them. Two died the
next. He replaced these. A puppy chewed up three, two of
them beyond repair and one bitten down to the graft.[1] The
third broke into leaf at points far from orthodox, but survived.

Pruning vines is a challenge. The second year with his little
book, his seccateurs and a big breath, he got this over in a
morning. He had to be restored with glasses of *grappa* before
lunch. The third spring was trickier, for vines in their first years
must be pruned by their ages, and he now had them of two
ages, and the next year, of three. The results were more
unorthodox than ever, and he was tempted to throw a
tarpaulin over the lot if any vine-growing friend arrived: but
grapes grew. At his first harvest he gathered about 80 pounds.
He ate nearly all himself.

The same way the soil was prepared for roses. Never
having planted a rosebush, he expected to wait a year or two
for results as with a fruit tree: so with amazement he greeted
his first bloom, of *Belle Blonde*, two months after planting.
This comes from the Meilland stable in France, and like others
was still in bloom for Hogmanay. *Soraya* was already at work

---

[1] Since 1863 all european vines, although phylloxera came to us from America,
have been grafted on certain american vine stocks which are resistant to this dread
trouble.

on new shoots in the middle of the following january; and the pearly buds of *Grace de Monaco* (who in her third year reached over 8 feet high) stayed after the frosts and into pruning time. By april all ten were in bud again.

By now the olives needed attention. To build the house only two olive trees and the little wild peach had to fall. The fourteen or fifteen left had been neglected for ten years and were tangled in airlessness unsunned and unventilated. The first year he got only two sacksful of fruit, about 160 pounds, which he took to the *frantoio* (press) in the nearest village.

It is about midwinter by the calendar when olives are crushed, and to go from the cold air into this ground-floor cellar of an old farmhouse is like going inside a gigantic heated olive skin. The odour of sweet ripeness, unimaginable to those who know only a thin liquid from a bottle, seems to splash off the walls and rafters—but not from the floor, which is cleaned after each crushing. Everything else is damp with odour and oil. One touch, and hands must be rinsed under a cold water tap in a wall. You come out clothed in olive.

Farmers have been there since earlier morning, shouldering their sacks from carts by the latched door, unless they are part of a great estate, in which case the sacks slide down a chute from lorries. Any farmer with enough for a whole crushing has this to himself: otherwise they inspect each other's harvest and go in with neighbours.

In a big cement drum two huge vertical millstones rumble round, driven by electricity, and turn the black fruit into mud-coloured granular mush. A trapdoor opens in the drum's side, and the mush is smeared on a round rush mat, which turns a complete circle, while a scraper smoothes it like pastry for a pie. While the farmer's boy prepares to lay another mat, the farmer himself lifts off the first one and lays it on a circular trolley. In the middle of this a vertical fat steel tube fits into a hole in the middle of the mat.

Mat follows mat. As the pile grows, an extension is fitted to the tube. When the tower so made is head-high, a polished curved cone like the nose of a torpedo is clamped on the tube top. The tower of mats and mush is then trundled over to the press. But already olive oil is oozing from the lower mats into a runnel round the base, because each fourth layer is not mat but heavy disc of steel.

The nose fits into a socket which comes down from the top of the press with an imperceptible pressure. The stanchions on either side resemble an old-fashioned printing press. Now the oil trickles freely into the runnel, from which it flows into a container. Being full of crushed twigs, stones, and other un-recognisable impurities, the dirty brownish oil is strained in the container, and then pumped up to a tap from which it falls in a slow steady column of yellow-green virgin oil.

The oil from these fields is among the best in Tuscany, and infinitely better than some commercial mixtures sold abroad as Lucca oil. Not everyone likes it sweet like this. Some farmers give a tang to it by putting in those small leaves which a conscientious grower takes pains not to pick nor even to damage, since olive trees are not deciduous.

The yield from those two sacksful was $13\frac{1}{2}$ litres, or just under 3 imperial gallons of oil. Great was the moment when the family put it on bread which had been salted a little and rubbed lightly with a clove of garlic, to sample the first firstling of their own home-gathered olives.

But there had been another ceremony first. In the dark, scrupulously clean crushing shed, as each crushing goes forward, the owner of the previous one is finishing in a corner at a small table a kind of traditional token feast with his helpers, the press mechanic, the next waiting party, anyone who is there. The food is simple, usually bread and *salume*[1] apples, ham. But two little nuns, come to supervise their yield, provided home-made meat pies, *schiacciata* and their

---

[1] A generic name for all *salami* (italian sausages) and other cured products.

own gentle, sincere wine. This quiet sharing, in the sweet-sour green odour of olive has a slightly solemn side to friendliness, as before an air-raid.

At home the olive trees needed drastic pruning. They got it, from an elderly farmer who years before received a diploma for the pruning of olives. Whole limbs were truncated with an axe, boughs reduced with a billhook, branches and suckers eliminated. Branchlets were carefully trimmed and thinned with seccateurs for the fan formation that balances and lightens. Each tree looked like a lamb shorn in a rainstorm.

The gardener followed the farmer from tree to tree, watching his principles turning manual. So he came to recognise each tree. For olives are like human beings. Roses may respond to the counting of buds on a stem: no olive is like any other, and never has been. Some fruit on upward stems, some on downward growing ones: some stems must be trained for growth, others for fruit. The four original varieties of tree have become down the centuries as multiple as the congregations of the denominations of the presbyterian church. Each has to be handled according to its nature like children in a class. Like Florentines.

This next season the yield from the few remaining branches in the garden was very small: and the gardener lost most of that. He had taken his family to a friend's in Austria for Christmas, leaving the harvest in sacks for the farmer to carry to the *frantoio*. Most of them took mildew. He did not know that olives must not be kept in sacks, but spread on threshing floors or in chip-trays from the greengrocer, continually turned, until the crushing plant can accept them. This year he got 5 pints.

But the trees were in good heart again, and he took over the pruning himself. The following season 150 kilograms of fruit yielded 7·6 gallons. The next, when other farmers werr lamenting a poor season, 110 kilograms yielded nearly 5½ gallons. Later, with only 13 trees in bearing, he took 11 gallons of oil. By this time his friends were saying he was dotty about olives. As he was.

For the rest of the garden, there was no doubt that his mixture was fertile. In neglected ground wild oats grew $4\frac{1}{2}$ feet tall: an escaped lettuce crowned its 5 feet 8 inches of stem with a blue flower like chicory. A radish left in the ground till Hallowe'en measured 12 inches by 10 and weighed a pound and a quarter. It decorated a stuffed witch for the party. And clumps of Rudbeckia, divided from two survivors of the experimental bed and replanted outside the house, were trees of gold over 10 feet tall, shooting flames of gold into the olive air they floated on.

But he still got shocks. Digging to make small vegetable and herb gardens behind the house, he struck solid rock at one spit deep. He made terraces for these and for the annuals.

The only annuals that grew really well were flowers that grew wild in the fields anyway: calendulas, love-in-the-mist, poppies, snapdragon. Real garden flowers were as rare as orchids: a real botanist's delight! His particular bane was *ageratum houstonianum*, which he wanted because it was blue.

Never having used a seedbox, he took great trouble. The seeds germinated in a chip-tray. He thinned them out. They made no growth. This did not surprise him.

One authority said, Sow under glass. Another said, In a hot-bed. He had made a hot-bed for basil and *mimosa sensitiva*, and there was no more room. As glass he had used a mildly heated room. Now he put the seedbox near the window. The may sun burned the seedlings like straw. He decided not to try ageratum again till he knew more about more.

One october morning in the open corner of the back of the house which he used as potting-shed, tool-shed and to sit on a nailed-together stool, he found a big coarse blue flower awaiting him on the mud path. It was an *ageratum houstonianum*. He felt badly about this.

Nor were the herbaceous plants any happier, except for one

or two, aquilegia and *achillea filipendula* whose high yellow pancakes bravely spread and endured as dried decoration at Christmastime. He planted two fuchsias, which his friends said would not survive the first, waterless, summer's sun. They did not survive the first frost.

Also much of the ground about the house was nothing but builders' rubble. He exploited this, laying a little soil over tins, bottles, mortar lumps, broken bricks and wire: in which he grew cactus and agave and other fleshy plants. That these flourished was little due to him; for Sempervivums grew wild all over the banks and stony places, and *sedum acre* like a weed everywhere. A friend even made a small lawn of it, by cutting off the stems and leaving them to root into a carpet.

He decided to put the emphasis on ornamental trees, which he preferred anyway. The first was a tulip tree. One catalogue said, Plant in the sun; another, Plant in the shade. Having no shade, he put it in the sun, in an exposed place to please arriving friends. Alas! the difference in Tuscany between sun and shade is the difference between tropical and arctic. The tulip tree he planted in may was dead by september. He replaced it with a Catalpa. This arrived about 12 feet long. It is still there, but so high that no arriving friends can see the exquisite flowers, nor anything but stem.

He made a curve of six dogwood trees, for their foliage. Misreading the instructions, he cut off all the new bent branches, which set them back several years. Two died of frost. Near a third he found an ant's nest, one of scores in his garden, which he filled with a powder. It killed the dogwood tree that night.

Ants swarmed everywhere: gigantic, big, middling, little, miniature. Red, brown, black. Big headed, pin headed. Some nested in olive trees. He eliminated these. Then he found that this breed had been his best ally against olive fly.

The powder, though it killed trees, did not kill ants: it demoralised them. It was not in their standing orders. There was no precedent for it. They ran frenziedly in confusion. They ran away.

When he sowed radishes, no sooner had he set a seed, than it walked off. All of them, in a procession. He ran to fetch the powder and returned to find no seeds left. He sowed more, sprinkling them with the powder. One or two still got into motion, sturdy as heavy lorries under snow. He had to isolate the whole plot before re-sowing.

Is there space to talk of all the trees he planted? *Gingko biloba*, the strange chinese survivor from prehistory, which he had always wanted since seeing it in autumn glory in the Chelsea Apothecaries' Garden. It flourished, but the leaves never turned really gold before they fell off, and it bore neither flower nor fruit.

The little *Magnolia stellata*, with its delicately-tinted star-shaped flowers, much more friendly than the classic magnolias that abound in Florence. *Prunus pissardi ceratoflora*, the chinese cherry-plum, with purple leaves, red flowers and fruit, which are good to eat, if no rivals to italian cherry or english plum: a pomegranate, covered with blossom but never a fruit: a medlar: another fantastic chinese tree called *Rhus typhinus laciniata*. This is covered with soft suede like young stags' antlers. It has long ash-like leaves which go orange in autumn and it makes crimson cones which stay on the branch-tips all winter, like bloody grenades.

At the entrance to the property as gateposts he set a pair of *Poncyrus trifoliata* trees. These are the original bitter orange of the Orient. The yellow-green thorns are much longer, stronger and more spiteful than those of a citrus, and are said to have been what the Crown of Thorns was made of. Geographically this is unlikely: but they are certainly the thorns depicted in religious pictures and stuck on plaster images, especially those of the nineteenth century. Little white balls of blossom open into something like that of the cultivated orange, and turn into small green fruits no bigger than large

98

chestnuts, colouring on the branches to overlap with a new generation of flower. These trees, with roses, cactus, pyracantha, agave and groundrows of purple berberis made a prickly welcome which most guests forgave.

He planted a cross between a persimmon and an apple, two almond trees of the *seccarella* variety with soft shells that do not need a sledge-hammer, and several kinds of cistus. But almonds proliferated all over the view from the garden and cistus grew wild on the edges of the woods.

The best of his ornamental trees were the climbers, along the speckly stone wall from the garage to the house. First came winter jasmin to tint the wall in winter: a novelty to his friends. Then a wistaria, which as a specimen even the nurserymen admired. Next came *Periploca graeca*, in whose serpentine twists rise square flowers of green and brown like midgets' cushions. And after that, always in order of flowering, *Physianthus albens*, also called Araujia, an exotic native of Brazil. This puts out sensually perfumed white, hyacinth-like flowers, which moths drink from till they stupefy and die. Macroglossum moths especially with their long probosces. If you dislodge them, they fall back in a daze and clamber slowly back in a dream to their drug. Within a day they are dead, still sucking, gummed to their chosen or conditioned destiny. The fruits that follow are like corrugated green nuts, up to 5 inches long, shaped like a bobbin of wound wool. Inside, the fruit is like a green-yolked hard-boiled-egg, the vivid green lying in strands of silvery glinting silk: for which reason it is sometimes called the Silk Tree. He touched the fruit with his tongue and immediately went to rinse his mouth. It was warningly bitter.

In the shade of an olive tree by the entrance to the house, he planted *Clematis montana rubens*, the pink-flowering kind. A stray dog which stayed with him for half a year not only ate most of the bulbs he had planted but chewed through the stem of this, about a foot above the ground. The family wept, for the clematis had done well; and the runt, trimmed off with seccateurs, was left in the ground till it could be replaced the following spring. The results of this involuntary and monstrous pruning were sensational. Instead of dying, the clematis vines spread across the front door, along the speckled wall, over the kitchen door and half round the side of the house with blossoms every 2 or 3 inches.

And then the weeds. On the heels of the giant medick he had eradicated literally with the sweat of his brow, came couch-grass. On the heels of the eradicated couch-grass, creeping clover. Flower roots were choked by scarlet pimpernel, appearing overnight in mats. Fennel, with roots like ropes, survived the waterless summers which flowers could not. Insects, fungoids, cryptogams, viruses proliferated.

Italy is an insectologist's paradise and a gardener's inferno. From turnipfly to greenfly and rosechafer, from black lice on chrysanthemums to red lice on roses, bugs are as numerous as blossom. There are no birds to eat them. Chemical firms prosper: one mixture of two patent fluids for a peach tree; another for a rose; vines need several treatments at once. If one went by all the advice a potting-shed would be a dispensary.

But he had little money, and what he had went on elementary tools.

His first spade turned up from the hard earth and reproached him. When he asked a farmer if this were the usual behaviour of spades, the reply was: '*Madonna*! what strength!' He bought a hoe and another spade, but nobody would sell him a handle. He had to go into his part of the wood and cut himself poles.

When there was water in the main, its pressure burst the plastic hose. After binding up twenty leaks, he went and daringly bought a decent rubber one. From then on, the water supply failed.

His pet tool was his trowel. After the first year this had a lip curled like a cockled sheet of paper.

In spite of all this, he did shape something like a garden, in which he was most proud of the herb-garden.

This he designed in quadrangles between rosemary and lavender. Rosemary is much used for flavourings, and the stems of lavender are bent over the heads and tied with thread, making cigar-shaped sachets prettier than those of chiffon. These bushes grew so thick and broad that before long there was little room for a herb-garden inside. But he persevered. He devised patterns, diagonals, parallels, key-patterns, saltires, squares. It was easier to design than to peg them out, he found. One peg was a sharpened piece of wood used by the builders more than a year previously. Within a month or two it grew two pairs of olive leaves. He left this miracle for all to see. But the miracle went back to peg.

Not knowing how big a salvia plant would grow, and wishing plenty for flavouring, he planted three. They filled their square and suffocated the thyme round them. The thyme did not mind; it merely transplanted itself to the brick paths. Such he used in salad dressings, and marjoram, which he planted, too. Also basil from Genoa, which makes the best basil and uses it, as his wife did, for making *pesto*, a special sauce for pasta asciutta, typical of Genoa and that part. He grew rue to put in bottles of *grappa*, and also because it is said to be good against stings. He grew borage for summer cups of white wine: and coriander to give an aromatic flavour to potted fish.

In the other half of the herb-garden he grew more eatable things, little round sweet melons with a rind that looked like a net; the yellow flowers of these were populous with lady-birds, and often their young. He let them be. Who would murder a ladybird, even if it reduces fruiting? Especially a young one.

He grew those extra things that make all the difference to salads. Special dandelions, which when young have delicious leaves, *erba stella*, chervil which tastes lightly of aniseed, melissa, pimpinella, minutina. He tried and rejected rocket, which tasted of rubber. Once he tried horse-radish, which is unknown in Italy with beef or without: the little carbon sticks just disappeared. He tried also samphire, which goes well with steamed fish: but that was foolish of him, for it likes sea air. The products of the herb-garden reached their climax and corona, when his wife, nostalgic for an english sausage, made fresh ones with minced pork, thyme, sage and marjoram.

But all this makes me aware that I am hungry. Since the tale has no end, let us stop it here and talk of what the Florentines eat and drink.

14

Florentine Food and Drink

Considering that Italians were the first sophisticated cooks in Europe and more highly prized by french gourmets than Frenchmen were at the time of the Renaissance and after; and considering that Florence in the early Renaissance was not only the chief centre of the new culture but also the city most advanced in agriculture, business, domestic economy, statistics, and other realistic sciences: it is surprising that she was not more inventive in so realistic a form of culture as cooking.

The fact is that in comparison with Modena, Bologna, and other cities of her size or smaller, and even with her rival Venice, she has contributed little to gastronomy. Her own dishes are few and have grown from early tastes but without developing much.

Most famous, I suppose, is the Florentine Steak[1], which may have gone to the United States as a 'T-steak': a sirloin split sideways an inch thick and usually grilled. For the gourmand, the bigger the better: but for many people what we call the undercut is enough, which is always more tender and sweeter.

Mutton is not eaten in Italy, or not generally; and lamb is killed very young indeed. I wish I could claim that tuscan *agnello* is better than roman *abbacchio:* but this would not be true, for no lamb I ever tasted has equalled that.

Roast wild boar meat comes in season from the Maremma, down the tuscan coast. This is a very large marshy tract which

---

[1] Not to be confused with *rosbif* which Italians offer to british visitors as a little bit of home. This is a lump of beef folded and trussed and cut in discs as thick as a pork chop.

extends nearly to Rome. The Etruscans had drained it, but in the middle ages it became a malaria swamp again and was deserted. Recent drainage schemes and land settlement have turned much of it into first-class farming land, but there are still areas to hunt wild boar in. Wild boar meat is gamey, but can be rather tough. I don't think there is any specially tuscan way of cooking it, or indeed any other meat, except perhaps the frying of pork chops in good olive oil and fennel, to which water is added later.

Fennel is by no means limited to, but is much used in, Tuscany, either as a cooked vegetable or raw in salads. For salads a special type is grown, the taste being of aniseed and the crunch that of celery. At the end of medicean banquets everybody chewed a flake or two, to round off the experiences of the palate as we sip coffee: and for centuries, perhaps even to this day, so clean is its flavour, that it has been used by wine-tasters to purge the mouth between different wines. It has indeed the reputation of bringing out latent possibilities in even indifferent wine, which could be palmed off on purchasers this way. And so the italian word for 'to enfennel' has come to mean subtle fraud.[1]

In the matter of flavouring one has to be careful of one's cook. Many, not trusting a natural flavour, over-stuff meat, chicken, and even the blue trout from the Appennines with rosemary, parsley, thyme, sage, or other herbs. This applies also to *salmi* of hare, which is sometimes too peppery for any but an addict of indian curry. It applies to most fish.

Florence being halfway between the Tirrhenian and Adriatic seas can choose fish from either. Soles are held to be better from the Adriatic: so are red mullet, because they are[2] larger

---

[1] How do we come to abuse vegetables, fruits and flowers? Fennel in italian has a sense like that of the russian little-garden-strawberry, or the english pansy.

[2] By some considered the most palatable of all fish. It tastes faintly of lobster. I have never had a true lobster in Florence. What are sold as such are in my experience crayfish, and none the worse for that. The true lobster, with claws, does exist in the Mediterranean.

and easier to dissect. Many fish in the Florence markets are unknown in northern seas, but fully the equal of herring, turbot &c.: *muggine*[1], roast tunny steaks, *ombrina*, *orata*, *dentice*, to name a few, and the big *San Pietro* from the Adriatic. The little tiddlers in the Arno are good in a *fritto misto*.[2]

To me fresh whole anchovies are much better than those salted fillets which arrive in Britain; but these too are good on bread and rolls. Fresh sardines are regarded as food for cats.[3]

One of the best tuscan fish dishes is mussels, cooked in oil, parsley, garlic and tomatoes, and eaten as if half-open hot oysters. Another takes its name from Livorno, an hour and a half's run from Florence, which is almost any fish done with origanum, tomato and other herbs: when cayenne pepper or chilli are added, this becomes the highly piquant *cacciucco* of the tuscan coast.

I know of no special tuscan vegetable nor way of serving it. Globe artichokes[4] rival those of Latium but are not so plump. Globe artichokes in Italy are never the overgrown bombs of England, prickly as thistles, of which the sucked leaves tear the gums and only the disc is good to eat. In Italy they are cooked young and whole, only a few outer coarser leaves being stripped. Tiny ones under oil or vinegar go well with cold meat or cold chicken in the company of olives, gherkins, and their pickle cousins.

But all vegetables are better treated in Italy, where carrots are small and made of carrot-flesh not wood, and peas are peas not marbles filled with flour. (Scarlet runners would be given to donkeys.) Also all vegetables come from the local farms

---

[1] Also called *cefalo*, or blue mullet: a very distant cousin of the red, bigger and less bony.

[2] Always of fish in Italy. Usually containing sepias, small octopus and other creatures that make british thoughts shudder: but well cooked they are tender and delicious.

[3] But if they are gently done in butter, I become a cat.

[4] Jerusalem artichokes are unknown in Italy except in Piedmont, where they are called sunflowers. Which indeed they are.

to the market laboratory-clean with no earth even on potatoes.

Vegetable marrows, too, are cut when half the size of bananas, and either boiled, or sliced and fried in batter, or stuffed with meat filling. An italian cousin of my wife's makes these last so well that I, who prefer quality to quantity except if they go together, once cleared two serving-dishes of them. The flowers of vegetable marrow, removing which is no waste as the body forms behind the flower, are, when fried in a batter as light as themselves, the most fragrant vegetable outside China.

We have the usual southern vegetables like aubergines and peppers green, yellow, or red. We steep the aubergines in salt before washing and cooking them, which gets rid of the bitterness. The latter make a splendid dish called a *peperonata*, in which they meet tomatoes, onions, lard and butter.

Italians envy us our supply of tomatoes all the year round, because in Italy one gets fresh tomatoes only in season. This is surprising in view of the number of italian dishes that contain tomatoes. But in season they are so plentiful that they can be tinned or made into conserve at little cost and so remain cheap, at least for cooking, throughout the year. Foreigners are sometimes puzzled by the big green tomatoes in shops. These are sliced for salads: not quite so succulent as red, sun-ripened ones, but fresh and refreshing. As refreshing, though little known, are plain tomatoes, peeled and squashed with nothing else as an accompaniment to *pasta al burro*[1] on hot summer days.

The soups of Italy are far from limited to 'Minestrone,' of which there are many varieties. Tuscany makes two special ones, of beans, and of chick-peas.[2] I've had also a notable one

---

[1] *Pasta* (preferably spaghetti) served quite plain with a lump of butter to dissolve in it on the plate. The delight of epicures tired of *sugo* or forbidden it.

[2] For those who are not skipping this chapter: the former is made with onion, cabbage, garlic, tomato juice, leeks, bacon and olive oil; the latter from onions, lard, marjoram, rosemary.

of small crayfish, rice, one or two vegetables, laurel leaf, brandy and white wine. And akin to soups are *pappa di pane* and *ribollita*, which are bread made into a kind of sop, the former much more attractive than it sounds.

Italians treat tripe more ceremoniously than Lancastrians. They cook it in an elaborate rich *sugo* for hours, so that the flavour impregnates the tripe itself: but here I find the roman way better than the florentine.[1]

In parenthesis, there is an odd gastronomic difference between Scotland and Italy. In the former sweetbreads are a luxury and brains despised, while in Italy brains cost more than sweetbreads. They are splendid when fried in butter and white wine. So, if I may shock the reader, are genitals, which I had for the first time the other day by accident. Sliced fine and fried, these have the flavour of sweetbreads and the consistency of cod's roe.

(And parenthesis within parenthesis: smoked roe can be found in Italy as *bottarga*.)

But France has outrun Italy in her own direction. Italians cannot make omelettes or soufflés, and it is not fair to ask them. Their *frittata*, which they sometimes call *omelette*, is more like a flourless pancake, and good. They do not like sauces, though they often use a white sauce which Louis XIV's famous inventor would not recognise as a *béchamelle*.[2] They are not good at cakes, pastry or biscuits, and what good sweets they have are of french origin. The amount of starch they consume in *pasta* makes sugar diatetically less necessary than in colder countries. But Siena makes its *panforte*, which is not unlike a flattened Black Bun—and eaten at the same season. And there are a few minor dainties made in Florence.

On certain feast days you can buy from street barrows

---

[1] The tuscan sort uses tomato sauce and meat extract, the roman sort vegetables, cheese, cloves and laurel leaf.

[2] Louis Bechamel, who is described by various authorities as a rich banker and as Louis XIV's *maitre d'hotel* (he may have been both) invented this basis of a multitude of, if not of all, french sauces.

little biscuits called *brigidini*, which are not very sweet, but are made with butter: also with aniseed and marsala: and forged into discs by hot tongs. In autumn and early winter there are sweetish flat cakes of chestnut flour, called *castagnacci* which contain raisins and pine kernels. During Lent there is *rosmarin*, rosemary bread, a little like the scottish currant loaf. And at all seasons Florentines munch their *schiacciata*: sections of a flat bannock made with lard, not unlike a neapolitan pizza (the word sometimes given to it) but with nothing on top but salt. They buy usually two sections, at any hour of the day from early morning onward, one to eat in the shop and another to chew walking.

Their *antipasti* as a rule do not approach french *hors d'oeuvre* for variety. Salume, olives black or green, ham raw or boiled, and *croûtes* of chicken liver not on toast but on bread: these are all. But over the merits of a serving of raw ham opinions can differ almost to duelling point, as with the French over a *pâté de maison*.

It was a shock to me in my early years here to see in a shop a ham marked *stravecchio*, a term, equivalent to V.O., applied to old brandy and tuscan cigars. Many are the claims of different regions: some say that the sweet hams of Parma or of San Daniele near Venice are the best in Italy: others prefer the home-cured tuscan, which is saltier. Any italian ham can be cooked (and sometimes York and Philadelphia must look to their laurels) or eaten raw. If raw, it must be cut thinner than smoked salmon[1] and cut with the knife along the curves of the tiny sinews. This can be taken by itself, or with slices of melon (no sugar, ginger, or anything else) or with ripe figs: in which case it will be exquisite. If it happens to be wild boar ham, it is unequalled.

Val d'Arno chickens are as famous to epicures as those of southern Burgundy: and chicken is as common as veal here. It is divided into quarters, as a rule, unless it is fried, in which

---

[1] Which is better cut thick, anyhow.

case it is smashed with a hammer, making bone-fragments somewhat dangerous. If divided for more than four, the wing is the least appreciated portion, because no sections of breast go with it. In Florence and the neighbourhood chicken breasts are a cheaper dish than meat. What happens to the rest of the bird, I have never found out.

But some of these and other delicacies are not to be found in restaurants. For *roventini* one must frequent the poorer quarters with their *rosticcerie*.[1] One must live in Florence to sample all her mushrooms, since only *porcini* are sold in the market. The *porcino* is a boletus usually grilled and sometimes so big that it covers the whole plate. Unless notice is given, it may be over-seasoned.

But there are many other edible mushrooms. The cultivated mushroom tends to be as dull as those in England, although in the field above where we now live, until it was ploughed up, we used to find the real horse-mushroom, firmer and less slimy than the *porcino*. There are *pineroli*, which grow under pinetrees. And, much more important, there are *bubbole*. *Bubbole*, or to fungologists *Lepiota procera*,[2] have very tall stems and at first round, blobby heads, so that they are sometimes called 'Drum-sticks.' When the heads turn flat, they are covered with rather unappetising squamoid patches. But whoever rejects them, misses a treat; for to me they excel all mushrooms I ever tasted. Of course there are several smaller mushrooms like *chanterelles* (called 'Little coxcombs'), which are found mixed in country dishes. And if a greengrocer dries his own, they are likely to rival almost those of Poland.

Lastly, cheeses. Italian cheeses do not any longer necessarily come from their places of famous origin. The sweet, creamy Gorgonzola, more gracious than Stilton, is now made in

---

[1] A kind of hot buffet. In some you can also sit at table: and a few are indistinguishable from a trattoria. *Roventini* are slices of black pudding spread with grated cheese and folded into a bread roll.

[2] *Procer* (noble, or chief) would have been the latin description of the head of a highland clan if Antonine or Agricola had ever dared to meet any.

places far from the mountain village of *I Promessi Sposi*.[1] Parmesan, when called Reggiano, is made in Reggio Emilia not Parma itself. But in all Italy there is no *pecorino*, no sheep's milk cheese, to equal that of Siena, where alone it is made round, low, friendly, delicate and aromatic. Even Romans on holiday in Tuscany buy whole ones to take home.

But I cannot leave this section without a word about plain beans. The *civaiolo* shops have sackfuls of these in many varieties of size and colouring. The variety whose flower in England can drape perfume across a motorway on a fine may morning, is so popular here, not cooked, that if you leave a bowl of it on a sideboard, and a visitor comes, you will find only empty pods left when he goes.

If this chapter is sounding too much like a cookery book, I am impenitent. Food can be as much a part of locality as speech or any other form of custom, and like them is best appreciated in it. Oatmeal, *pasta*, *shashlik*, *arroz con pollo*, however expertly prepared, do not taste quite the same in isolation as they do in the countries where they are plentiful and where preparation is a birthright: just as a wine which may be feckless in another country or another part of its own country can be right and belong with a dish of its own locality, certain white wines with their own sea food, for example.

And so we come to drinks.

I imagine the largest drink sales in Italy are of bottled mineral water. Many people take it with *pasta*, thereby helping the liver, Italy's weakest bodily organ—perhaps because so much *pasta* is swallowed with so little chew. Almost every big town has its local spring, since no town in Italy is far from a hill: and so has its local brand, which varies from its neighbours only in degrees and diversities of mineral saltiness. Tuscany has several.

Tuscan wine is known to most people outside Italy through

---

[1] Classic italian novel by Alessandro Manzoni, published from 1825–7. It has languors even to an assiduous reader.

the name Chianti, because that not immense area produces much. The wine of the inner circle of the region, which sells at higher prices, has been known since 1932 as *Chianti Classico*, and carries a label with a black cockerel. This inner circle extends from just south of Florence to just north of Siena, about 200 square miles of hills and vineyards.

The circle outside gives wines which are also called *Chianti* but not *Classico*. They are made from Arezzo to Pisa, from Pistoia to Poggibonsi, a parallelogram, if my reckoning is right, of about 2,400 square miles. The different subdistricts of this have their wine labelled with a chimera, a bunch of grapes, a red lily, a centaur, the roman she-wolf, the towers of Montalbano, or a *putto* (cherub). The *putto* is the sign of florentine *chianti*, and also of that made in Rùfina, a small town on the Sieve, which is a tributary of the Arno above Florence.[1]

All these *chianti* wines can be divided into two types. The majority is intended to be drunk within the year, and so made, by an old tuscan method wherein a few grapes are added after fermentation to use up sugar. I have read that to this end the *chianti* straw-covered flasks with the long necks and the straw twist for collecting empties have a functional shape. It is a great pity that commercial growers and vendors have recently abandoned straw for hideous surrounds stamped out of plastic and meaninglessly decorated.

A smaller quantity is made for ageing, and after years in the wood is put into bottles not flasks. It is an even greater pity that the growers' associations have recently adopted bottles that remind one of Coca-Cola, an insult to what can be dignified and distinguished wines.[2]

All present-day *chiantis* are the result of successful experiments over a hundred years ago by Baron Bettino Ricàsoli (one of the principal founders of the italian nation in 1860)

---

[1] Not to be confused with Ruffíno, which is the name of a wine factory at Pontassieve.

[2] To british readers interested in italian wines I strongly recommend Cyril Ray's exhaustive book *The Wines of Italy* (London 1966).

using four types of italian grape. A mature wine of good vintage from his lands at Broglio can be well set beside a fine Rhône wine: but so can other *chianti classici.*

In the main the red is better than the white, which to me too often comes heavy and surly: but this does not mean that there are not fragrant and delicate white *chiantis.* One is the same Baron's *Arbia* (accent on the first syllable) near Siena. Another comes from Ripalta in the valley of the Agliena after patient expert study and experiment by its proprietor. From the main valley of this area comes a *Vin Santo* said to be among the best in Italy.[1]

But tuscan wine was drunk with relish by connoisseurs long before Ricàsoli. The bacchic poet Francesco Redi in the seventeenth century called Montepulciano the king of all wines. In the most unexpected places one comes across really excellent wines, made in small quantities, unknown to commerce, even anonymous, by a chance stop at a wayside trattoria or at a friend's house in the locality. Thus there is a pleasant white wine near Grosseto, called Petigliano. There is another at Montecarlo near Lucca. And I have had a really pleasant wine made not by a vine-grower but by his young children from wine-grapes grown in the policies in a district not known for really good wines. Which shows that wine depends not only on the whimsies of soil[2] but also on the brain of the maker, his choice of grape and his skill (and luck each season) in making.

Grappa is a spirit distilled from grape-pips or sometimes from the dregs (*vinacce*) after pressing. It is better than italian brandy, which is hard and sweetish like that of Spain. But beware of grappa made in cities like Bologna or Florence! The real stuff comes from Veneto and Piedmont. It is clean,

---

[1] In Val di Pesa. *Vin santo* is made all over the peninsula as a dessert wine, or to take as we take sherry. It is said to derive its name from being made during Holy Week out of grapes dried on straw throughout the winter. (Cyril Ray.)

[2] The grower at Ripalta once showed me a field, divided by a sloping lane, of an apparently homogeneous soil. He could grow only red grapes on one side of the lane, only white on the other, with any success.

unliverish, unheadachy; nearer to good russian vodka than to brandy. Call it an *eau-de-vie*. Some put a spray of rue in the bottle. I grow my rue for that difference.

Not far from Florence is a monastery on a woody hill called Monte Senario, founded as a retreat by seven young florentine aristocrats, the *Servi di Maria*, who had just built the church of Santissima Annunziata and had it frescoed by artists as young as themselves. The present monks distil a liqueur called *Gemma d'Abete* (Fir Bud or Fir Jewel), sweet and aromatic, something like Glayva. The monks of S. Maria Novella make a sweet liqueur, Alhermes, best for flavourings, and a bitterish digestive one called Elixir di China. However, the best drink in Scotland is whisky, the best drink in a ship is rum. So also the best drink in Florence is tuscan wine, famous or humble, your own if you are lucky, if not, your neighbour's. And like all local drinks, at least alcoholic ones, it makes the local food taste better.

15

An Egg and A Leg

On a hill above Florence lived an old man who broke his leg. Faced with weeks of inactivity on his back, and chafing at being useless, he asked for a new-laid hen's egg to hatch.

The egg cooked under him; and a chick pecked out. It became the old man's pet and 'grandson.'[1]

When he was out of bed, but hardly able to walk, his son and daughter-in-law decided to take their young family for a picnic. They felt that with his disability at his age a trip in a car would be too difficult for the old man. So they left him at home.

They motored to Monte Senario, six miles and more away, walked in the woods, and settled to the picnic. They were in the middle of it, when they heard grandfather's voice plaintive among the trees: 'What! no food for an old man?'

He had walked the whole distance and thought nothing of it.

[1] This will be no surprise to readers of Thomas Hardy. Arabella Donn before she seduces Jude is carrying an egg in her bosom in (what is perhaps the bravest attack on the 'Establishment' ever written:) *Jude the Obscure* (1895).

16

Spring

Foliage in Tuscany throughout the year stays mainly glaucous with cypress and olive, the latter tipped bright silver under grey skies. There are no first spring sparks of crackling green except in roadside hedges, and hedges are few. In place of hedges are walls, which seem to lean back and inward as they curve down slopes: walls with dark rosemary so frequent that greengrocers do not stock it but advise you to go out and lift some: walls from which giant agaves jut out like public clocks. Only patches of deciduous trees like oaks, young shoots of umbrella pines, re-leafing of flowering ashes, gleaming green of young corn, announce the spring. Browning's lines about April in England[1], laughed at in England, assert his original meaning in Tuscany.

But in the corn the wild flowers are english garden treasures: wild tuscan anemones and pasque-flowers, wild tulips and pheasant-eye narcissus, jonquils, blood-pink gladiolus which are here called 'sword-blades.' Round hundreds of fields tramp the white or mauve irises called the 'florentine lily.' They smell of sweet paper, but their rhizomes like violets. From the rhizomes orris-root powder is made, which was much used in the manufacture of toothpaste and is better for the scalps of actors than face-powder on the hair. For which practical reason, and because they need no tending, these irises were encouraged on the edges of fields.

There are few signs that this crop is ever now taken: but

---

[1] *'Oh, to be in England*
Now that April's there!'

Florence remains the City of the Iris. A strong group of horticulturalists and garden-lovers holds an annual show of the cultivated iris at the Piazzale Michelangelo, with international awards. These generally go to Americans. For this reason there is some prospect that the show will be lost to Europe. Then flowers will follow books, manuscripts, works of art and furniture across the Atlantic to the Unnamed Empire.

Iris tuberosa, the small green and black 'widow' iris, is brought in by children from the fields each spring, where they find it in company with a striped clusiana tulip. At this time blossom creams over wild almond, peach and plum trees on edges of woods and farms. Soon tiny orchids, some of them fragrant, are found by keen eyes in rising pastures. Now there are grape hyacinths, daffodils that look like Crown Imperials, rock-rose, pennycress with discs full of tadpoles, and many variations on british wild flowers,—Baxbaum's speedwell, for example, more interesting to close botanists. Primroses, my flower, are rare.

Birds come into notice. Chaffinches, when they leave their winter clubs and seek family life, are not so bright as their northern brothers, and drop half a bar from their song. The italian sparrow, never so house-daring as ours, has the markings of both our kinds of sparrow. Blackcaps, which have wintered here, break into loud song, and other warblers, notably the Orphean, into lesser. Couples of goldcrests hunt insects in olive trees. Titmice, mostly ox-eyes, thump on their tinny anvils. As elsewhere it is the chiffchaff who arrives as first spring visitor.

But by comparison this is a silent countryside. No Tuscan sings in field or farm. Nobody plays guitar or accordion, still less a mandoline. If you hear a song in a street, it will come from radio or telly; if you see a music-case walking, it is on its way to give popular favourites in a tourist restaurant. Certainly in some city gardens you may hear bird song, which can eliminate solitude and take the jab out of anxieties. But it will be the song of refugees. In the country there are almost no resident songbirds. Any bird that sings, except the blackbird, which is mercifully fearfully black, is at once put to death and either left there, or cooked and eaten, or sold for less than sixpence.

This devouring of little birds, which have less flavour and bigger bones than frog-legs, is general in Italy. Even the great naturalist Paolo Savi in his book on tuscan birds follows his observations with advice on methods of killing and cooking them. Elizabeth Barrett Browning ate thrushes.

From plovers and doves to bullfinches, goldfinches, red-breasts and larks, they are laid out on counters at the entrance to eatingplaces and in poulterers' shops. Italy, say the eaters, is a poor country and must eat all it can. But this is not true. Workers' wives buy expensive meat in quantities. I have seen labourers enjoying wild boar and hare at Pontassieve. Deli-cacies are sold in working-class quarters that are sold also among the rich.

The wolfing of spitted birds is due not to poverty but to the depraved tastes of petty men who want to be potentates. It is due to what made Nero, pettiest of potentates, impress his guests with a pie of a thousand larks' tongues.

Not pleasant was the gloating grin on a young motor-cyclist's face as he stopped, swaddled and gun-slung like a ski-patrol Finn, outside Desiderio's bar at Settignano, and raised seven dead song-thrushes on a string for the admiring envy of his friends inside. Not very agreeable the reply of an agreeable florentine acquaintance, when asked why he obliterated birds, that every now and then he had a longing 'to take his gun for a walk.'

Not palate, but sense of power. They call themselves 'huntsmen' and the scratching of their itch 'the chase.' They dress up in a kind of lay uniform. Armies of them. They have taken the right to shoot anywhere, on private property, within fifty paces of a house, not turning their backs on it.

From dawn every morning in the season, but especially on sundays and holidays, and up till and even after dusk, they are allowed to pepper and drum their pellets on your windows. They shoot at anything that moves: birds, cats, dogs, children, even at each other. Not a week passes in the season but a 'hunting accident' is noted in newspapers. If they hear a rustle and suspect a hare, they form up in semicircles and volley their pop-guns like Brens. One even once had a pot at Maresa's Austin-Healey Sprite as she drove it through the wood. Maybe the marksman mistook it for some protozoic lizard. Another shot at me when I went out to protest only twenty-five paces from the house. He could have mistaken me for nothing else.

Only recently has this become a 'sport' in Florence. When hawking went out of fashion florentine citizens left winged game to the fowlers, whose livelihood it was. They used decoys and nets. Nets are now nominally illegal.

Such extermination of avian voices to the detriment of the tourist trade, such extirpation of avian beaks which damages agriculture, horticulture and husbandry, such targetless expulsion of shot that starts conflagrations and eliminates woods and vineyards,[1] does raise some objections among Florentines more sensitive and more sensible. An experiment was made some years ago in Capri (not without threats of personal injury to the organiser) to set apart a bird sanctuary. Later the whole island was protected. Now in other parts of Italy there are bird sanctuaries. But few: and as soon as their denizens come out for food or exercise, they are blazed at by lurking nimrods.

Protest groups are still in infancy. A national society has been formed to get government help in limiting the depradations of these Sauls and Davids:[2] and Tuscans too have joined

---

[1] It is significant that every year on the evening of the first day of autumn shooting Florence is ringed with forest fires that burn all night despite the efforts of several fire-brigades. These are caused less by cigarette-ends than by shot sparking from rocks in desiccated woods and left heedlessly to travel.

[2] *'Saul hath slain his thousands and David his tens of thousands.'*

it. But italian governments contain trigger-happy men or men with friends trigger-happy; and the society is as yet weak. It has, however, already achieved something. It has for instance caused the government to enquire whether it would be advisable or not, before a gun licence is issued, to ensure that the applicant knows how to use a gun. And it has made Rome anticipate the closing date of, and impose certain conditions on, spring shooting.

This last is important. But the motives are less an interest humane or agricultural on the government's part, than the huntsmen's fear of losing more birds than they could blow to pieces. Spring migrants were beginning to avoid the peninsula. We used to have several chiffchaffs together in our wood. Last year there was none.

So the little hitlers, without too much grumbling, consented to a five year armistice with the spring migrants—in the hope that by 1972 there will be a richer harvest of unsuspicious arrivals to reduce to carnage. In return they were conceded the retention of their death camps on the coast. The coasts of Tuscany and Liguria are as bird-bare as the woods and fields, even though waders and sea-birds which feed on fish do not make good eating to a normal palate; and Tuscans have normal palates. So any rare or common wing that flaps ashore will still be blown to pieces.

Spring song here, then, is the song of the lucky. Cuckoos and hoopoes have always arrived after the closure date. They assert and qualify all day long, the hoopoe's threefold note about a fourth below the second note of the cuckoo. Nightingales for the same reason are almost as numerous as the trees and bushes they sing from, till the sun gets too warm, and silence again empties the woods. With a blackbird in the lead, and a chaffinch or two, a redbreast, a great tit, birds do compose something like a dawn chorus. Only in this country it is more of a madrigal.

Yet Florentine people are not inhuman. If the skies of

London are filled with flocks of starling, if the skies of Rome with the aerobatics of swifts, then parts of the florentine sky, like parts of the venetian, are filled with the flutter of pigeons. A year or two back they became a public nuisance, especially in the Piazza Santissima Annunziata; and the local authority decided to reduce their numbers. It tried to do so with a diabolical sticky substance smeared on cornices, roofs and ledges. The birds were immobilised into death.

At once there was an outcry. Protests, letters to the press. So, sensitive, on this minor issue, to public opinion, the authority admitted its mistake and withdrew the glue. The nuisance goes on. Florentines accept it.

Is this chapter about spring written with heat? Has its writer let off too many and too heavy cannons at one side of the florentine spring? It is written by one who loves the spring. And birds. And Florence.

17

A Chapter on Games

This could almost be a chapter on the snakes in Iceland. Tuscans do not personally go in much for organised games. For which reason young boys of ten tend to too much puppy fat on legs and ribs, which does not always come off at man's estate.

In an open space by the Campo di Marte football ground, however, tall young men can be seen with tambourines of stretched sheepskin. With these a hard ball is hit into the air. It makes a noise like a rifle shot, soars 40 feet in air, makes a double parabola, lands with another bang on the tambourine of another player 40 yards away, and returns in another double parabola, to start again. There is no pitch. The skill needed for this game is something between that for badminton and a high catch at cricket.

Boys do practise dribbling, trapping, passing and heading soccer balls in imitation of professional heroes loved on television screens: and they are much more proficient than my contemporaries were at preparatory school. Also many a small town and village has its amateur soccer team and ground, which serve in local championships. But in the main a Florentine prefers to watch others at play.

He takes them fervently. His heart and mecca lie in Campo di Marte; and if Fiorentina is playing on its home ground, avoid all streets and bye-ways that lead near it on a sunday afternoon!

Fiorentina floats near the top of all-Italy contests and is often champion. Not only boys are its fans. Men, and women, in all classes, trades and professions, rule their free hours by it. A certain café favoured by its players has walls gay with its banner, signed photos, newspaper-cuttings of its glories: and fans throng there, calling their men by first name or nickname. But fans can also punish.

Once when Fiorentina had not lost a single match in a whole season, its last encounter was with Genoa, a team at that time weak. Fiorentina came home beaten ignominiously; and the motor-coach was surrounded by an infuriated and all but murderous mob, yelling insults and trying to assault their fallen gods and betrayers of dead-cert bets.

Each saturday every tobacco bar with the necessary accreditation is stiff with experts filling-in football coupons. Freak weather sometimes creates millionaires. But bigger chances of wealth come from the state lotteries, which four times in the year delegate part of the luck-choice to racing cars, race-horses or the most popular songs, new or old, at the San Remo festival.

Florence has her own horse races in the Cascíne; but this has a more limited and expert public. She stands in her streets when the Mille Miglia passes through: but this is a series of casual thrills rather than a dominant passion. Much more is she stirred by grim-faced cyclists, bearing on their vests the names of biscuit or vermouth manufacturers, who treadle past in the long Giro d'Italia. Then she writes preferred surnames on walls for the bowed heads to look up at, or on the asphalt for rubber tyres partly to rub out: a chalk cheer of encouragement.

This is the only form of chalk marking on roads. Children do play hop scotch, which they call 'little cripple' (*zoppino*) or sometimes 'the week' (*settimana*), but mostly in private.

Children's games are strangely international: which is part of the reason why international children can understand each other and co-operate without need of protocols, sanctions, bluffs, threats and wars, which adults have invented in their own personal interest. Hide and seek, puss in the corner ('*four corners*'), blind man's buff ('*blind fly*'), and various variations and developments like *guards and robbers*. Ring a ring o' roses is called *girotondo*, and is the first social action learnt by tots.

Children's card games are different. In Italy I don't think they play snap, nor beggar my neighbour, though the latter is not unlike *rubamazzo* (steal the pack). They have the 'black man,' which centres on the knave of spades, *briscola*, a sort of whist played also by adults, and merchant at the fair. In another way tuscan children differ from british: I have never seen or heard of the devilish slum game of last across the road. Maybe, in the chaos of italian traffic it was forbidden, even by Mussolini in spite of '*vivere pericolosamente!*'.[1]

The usual card games are played by adults in their homes or in cafés, and by the workers during the mid-day rest if they are too far away to get home. But these prefer the neapolitan pack to ours and a game called *scopa* (broom), fast and not easy for an outsider to follow: dramatic slams on the table: much jocularity: occasional tension: few recriminations: seldom a quarrel.

In Florence there is at least one billiard saloon: inside a café, unpublicised. There is no *casinò*:[2] and I doubt if there ever was. By contrast with England and even Scotland of today, where casinos bloom all over the place, there are only three or four left in Italy. This is not from puritanism. Florentines have something in common with the Scots, but not that puritanism which lingers in every Scot, making even an

---

[1] '*Live dangerously!*' a motto put forward by Mussolini in the hope of stimulating modern Italians to revive the glories of Imperial Rome. As a matter of fact, however, the motto of the Augustans would have been: 'Live richly. If you aren't rich, find a rich friend. In either case live comfortably.'

Modern Italians do follow Ancient Romans in *La Morra*, a game of chance and primitive mind-reading, on the number of fingers protruding from a flung hand. But this may have been played in Ur of the Chaldees, or indeed the Altamira caves.

[2] In Italy pronounce this word with a careful stress on the *last* syllable: otherwise people will think you are talking of a brothel. Brothels have been abolished, anyway.

emancipated one take his freedman pleasures with a squirm. A very upright and religious lawyer defended Norman Douglas when he was in trouble over a small girl in Florence, and managed to get the punishment limited to an order to leave the city. When asked later how he reconciled his actions with his convictions, the lawyer said: 'But the man was a genius. The ordinary rules of conduct do not apply.'

But if the non-puritan Scot does not as a rule back a hand of cards with coins, the non-puritan Florentine does not yearn for a flutter at the tables.

There is a golf course at a country club used mostly by foreigners. A few tennis-courts there are; but youths and girls walking home in shorts are never the common sight of the british suburbs. There are no bowling-greens that I know of, nor badminton courts, though I have seen what looked like a skittle alley.

The forms of exercise best liked are swimming and ski-ing, sea and snow being not so distant from Florence. Those who can afford it, disport themselves in the wire-fenced lidos which enclose beaches all down both coasts.[1] Those who cannot, patronise the two community bathing pools, or private ones in villa gardens if they have well-to-do friends. A surprising number of young workers are able to buy ski-ing outfits and join their richer competitors in the Appennines for week-ends and single sundays. Very few of these are 'cannibals' —the terrors of the *pista*, who swoop about knowing few rules, and disregarding those they do.

Croquet, I fancy, has quite died out. It must have existed; for Italians call it mallet-ball.

But Florentines have always preferred spectacle-sport to exercise-sport. The ancient football game may have been originally like that of Dorking: rival quarters of a primitive village doing bloody battle for a bullock's head: but by at

---

[1] If you find any spot in Italy where you can get to the sea to bathe without paying an entrance fee, you may well have to go down a cliff on a rope to reach it.

least the sixteenth century it had ceased to be a free-for-all and had crystallised into something like what visitors now see from their stands. The four quarters of the city still compete.

And the populace never took part in the jousts, though the same word in italian now applies to merry-go-rounds and other funs of the fair. Nor did the populace do more than look on at the *Palio dei Cocchi* on St John's Day, when four-horse chariots raced round the spots where the obelisks stand in Piazza Santa Maria Novella.

The strangest spectacle-sport in history, more worthy of Tartars or Homeric Greece than a civilised centre of Europe, must be the stampede of riderless colts through Florence's narrow streets, dangerous and thrilling as the Mille Miglia along the avenues, but meaningless, cruel and barbaric.

This took place every year from the time of Dante's grandfather till it was abolished at the time when Italy became a ninteenth century kingdom. It was called the Barbary Race, probably showing that the first steeds were Arabians. They were maddened by diabolic goads shaped like pears, so tied as to bite into their rumps; and they may have been doctored with alcohol. This crazed torrent pelted through the city from St Peter's Gate in the east, down what is now the Corso, through the Piazza della Republica as it now is, down the Vigna Nuova, along Ognissanti, and so out at the Prato Gate, where what was left of it was collected and driven home in pitiful condition. Side streets were barricaded off: but people were often injured, and many horses as a rule had broken legs and had to be destroyed.[1]

A social safety valve. The arena part of *panem et circenses*. Today it is Fiorentina at Campo di Marte or on the telly; and the cyclists. In improving on this piece of tradition by abandoning it, Florentines have not changed fundamentally.

---

[1] Boccaccio however seems to indicate that the course ran from the Prato Gate to St Peter's.

18

The Alpini Invasion

The Alpini hold reunions in different cities of Italy, like the scottish celts and their Mod.

The Alpini are a section of the italian army raised in 1872 as mountain fighters, like the french *chasseurs des alpes* and the austrian *alpensjäger*. They wear William Tell caps with a proud feather and rank among the finest regiments of the world. Fine to look at, too: lithe, agile, clean-cut, and mentally intelligent, self-reliant, disciplined (when necessary), gay.

Like the scottish and welsh celts, they sing. Like hebridean gaelic songs, theirs are reminders of sad events in glens or on braes, graceful love-songs, praise of mountain or meadow, or just rough humour. They sing always in harmony, sometimes three-part, but without a bass. When two or more are gathered together, they sing, forming a little knot.

One year they descended on Florence, thousands of them. The first thing the *Sindaco* did was to announce that any bar or shop which put up the price of liquor would be closed for ever. The Alpini, like the Gaels, are great drinkers.

Florence filled with smiles and song.

Their best choir gave a concert in the Signoría. All Florence tried to get in. A few hundreds succeeded. The piazza outside was thronged in the hope of hearing some song through the windows. The throng was not disappointed. Only a few dozen Alpini were in the Signoría: the rest in the throng with us. Little groups of them made knots, like stalls in a market, and sang whether people listened or not. People listened. They went from knot to knot to listen.

When the singing was over and the crowd dispersing, there was difficulty in crossing nearby streets, even on a zebra, because of the cars. At one corner a policeman watched but did nothing.

A young Alpino captain, seeing a pretty girl on the opposite pavement, held up his hand, stopped the cars, and crossed like an Israelite in the Red Sea.

'Signorina, would you care to cross the road?'

Hand up, and two Israelites crossed back to Egypt.

'And now would you care to cross again?'

Two Israelites re-crossed.

'And again, Signorina?'

There was no objection.

And again no objection.

'You see, Signorina, we are trying to cause a little confusion.'

But the signorina had seen the look in the policeman's eye, and refused further crossings.

That year we were living in Fiesole, and the third afternoon found the lower piazza full of Alpini. They had acquired an accordion and were dancing with the Fiesole girls. One of the rhythms was so like that of a scottish country dance, that we began to *pas-de-bas* together, into and among them. But I did not have my partner long. She was snatched away and vanished into mêlée and laughter.

That evening, having occasion to go to the grocer's,[1] I found a solitary Alpino reeling up the street and making weird drunken noises on a tuba or euphonium. Soberly the grocer said: 'You must excuse them, Signor Giuseppe. Up in the Alps there are no vines. When they come down to the plains, wine goes to their heads.'

---

[1] All shops stay open, after the mid-day closure, till 8 p.m. or later. A boon to housewives who are also in jobs.

'Do they never drink grappa?' I said, as gravely.

He did not reply.

A Florentine will always try to pull your leg if he likes you enough.

Even if he dislikes having his own leg pulled.

19

The Small Streets

The streets of Florence are unlike those of Venice, which reveal at every few yards perfect stage sets for Goldoni comedies readymade.[1] The streets of Florence are more pictorial. Not made so with that object: so made because useful so.

Apart from the wide avenues, open suburban walks, and pavements by fashionable shops (between which last there are often historic or beautiful old buildings), they are narrow: so narrow that the heavily projecting and timbered eaves, which seem like oblong companies or troops in plans of great battles, scissor the sky at street-ends and bends. These may seem affected; but there is no affectation. They launched heavy rain nearer to the middle of the walking way: and their usefulness is still known to whoever walks at summer midday in a metre of their shade on the pavement instead of being blistered by the vertical sun.

In the middle ages these streets were very likely further narrowed by stalls pushed out from the craftsmen's *botteghe*. Maybe these eaves sheltered also the goods on the stalls. The jostling, the heat or the sleet, the cold, the impatience of proud, full-blooded men, made walking unsafe. A knock could bring out a rapier, a trodden toe cause simultaneous deaths. I speak of the earlier city rather than Renaissance Florence, but urbanistically the two differ little. Many a

---

[1] The prolific dramatist Carlo Goldoni in eighteenth century Venice made human figures out of the harlequins, Brighellas, &c of the *commedia dell'Arte*, and created a comedy of manners important in the theatre history of Europe.

noble palace which went up between mediaeval houses and towers is still there in a narrow street between them.

The shapes of these streets cause thought, for they curve and meet in strange lines inexplicable without a little history. The Via Torta (*Bent Street*) bends because its houses were built on the foundations of the walls of the old roman amphitheatre. Even the façade of the House of the Peruzzi was bent for the same reason.

One or two *palazzi* still have their *loggias*, where great families shared their joys or griefs with their many dependants and the populace: a birth, a betrothal, a funeral, a dance; with free feasting afterwards. In the sixteenth century there were twenty-six of these. That of the Rucellai, across a little open space from the Palazzo Rucellai, has recently been opened up again, with panes of glass between the arches.

The impulse to share remains too. Still more recently the occupier of a *palazzo* on the Piazza Santa Trínita gave a banquet to 150 bigwigs. Having no *loggia*, he gave it in the piazza itself.

Borgo Santi Apostoli, which, being called a *borgo*, ran outside the great city wall, can take a studying person nearly half an hour to walk along, so much there is to see. Before it enters Piazza Santa Trínita, it also bends, because the great wall did. The noble battlemented Palazzo Spini bends the other way on that piazza, because it is part of, or built on, a bastion of that wall.

In the maze of small streets between Piazza Santa Maria Novella and the Via Tornabuoni there is a tiny space with a fourteenth century cross, called the Croce del Trebbio. There was some kind of bloody engagement or massacre in 1338, some century before the cross was set up, between traditional Catholics and the Patarini. The Patarini were part of a heresy called the Càthari. They were anti-feudal and anti-church-abuses: but they got out of their own control when ultra-left-wing members became anti-priest as well, and they were suppressed by the Church. In fact the Inquisition was set up to suppress them.[1]

This cross is less interesting than the row of ordinary houses beyond it, which curl away in an apparently meaningless curve. The curve may be due to one in the city wall, though this is not supposed to have wandered down that way. It is more likely due to the ditches which in this area brought in water for turning mills and washing wools. Nearby is the *Via dei Fossi* (Ditches Street) now a hunting-ground for fanciers of antiques.

Anyone who wishes in imagination to repeople Florence under Lorenzo de' Medici has only to walk 100 yards from the Duomo along Via Martelli, then called Broad Street, *Larga*; by comparison with the small streets of the people's city it seemed princely wide. The Medici Palace on the left is now the Prefettura, where the national governor of Florence maintains law and order and roman control. Its private garden at the back has shrunk to a backyard.

The houses on Broad Street are now quite different. There are shops and bustle and parking offences, all the way up the Via Cavour, which is its continuation. When he reaches Piazza San Marco, however, and looks left, he will see a florist's nurseries offering seeds, potplants, and young trees. This is the beginning of the large garden Lorenzo made for his sculptors and painters to study classical statues and talk. Most of the rest of it is built over.

It probably extended as far as the first turning on the left up Via Cavour. In the angle of the high wall there, if the time-traveller looks up, he will see a slim, lonely, barley-sugar twisted pillarette of white marble, with nothing on top but a

---

[1] There are people who think the Inquisition was the invention of Ignatius de Loyola and the Jesuits he founded. Certainly the Spanish Inquisition, bugbear in boys' adventure stories and brilliantly treated by Voltaire in *Candide*, did commit atrocities of torture. But the main Inquisition consisted of travelling inspectors, mostly Dominicans. who in fact once examined Ignatius himself.

shaped iron spike, rising as if the streets had been excavated round it. Behind stand very large holm-oaks. These may be descendants of trees Lorenzo saw. I cannot say that this pillarette is a survivor from the Medici garden, I think it comes from a later style: but it points.

In the parallel street, San Gallo, if you look through a gateway, you can see more large holm-oaks and a creditable green lawn with flowering shrubs. This too may be part of the same garden.

A young and promising Michelangelo frequented this garden, as did Leonardo da Vinci, before he was thrown out of his city, like Sophocles, for too blatant homosexuality. Leonardo's lodging was in a little house beyond the Medici Palace, more or less where a small church now stands back in a little piazza. These men and others still walk up from the Via Larga. One can see the people bowing as they pass with Lorenzo heavily bodyguarded: or maybe they went out through the back door, big and now blocked up, and along the then important street leading to the Porta San Gallo.

The names of Florence's streets are images in a historico-lyrical poem, which does not end with middle ages or Renaissance. Behind the Signoría is a short street called the Street of the Lions, because in 1550 living lions were kept there in symbol of florentine might: echoing the little stone ones, which sprout, against the rules of architecture, from the clustered columns of the Loggia dei Lanzi on the other side of the Piazza.

The smaller streets, lanes, alleys and corners (*vicoli, viuzzi, canti*) are even more socio-historical in their naming. Some, like the bigger streets, are still named after the families that lived there. Thus if a street were called *Via dei Cerchi*, it would mean the Street of Circles; but if *Via de' Cerchi*, the Street Where the Cerchi Family lives. There are both a *Via* and a *Vicolo de' Cerchi*.

Marchese Emilio Pucci, popular hero, politician, and fashion expert, sometimes gives his address thus: 'Easy: Emilio Pucci, Palazzo Pucci, Via de' Pucci, Firenze.'

Study the names of other lanes and alleys, and Florence starts up like the working models we came across in the Cascíne on the Day of the Cricket: Basin-makers' Alley, Stave-making Alley, New Mill and Blades' Alleys, Little Bog Alley, and the Lane of the Wee Furrier, Little Bower and Little Well Alleys, Bazaar Lane, Iron Lane, Lily Lane, Gold Lane, Silk Lane, Lane of the Wools.

When an alley is a cul-de-sac, it is called a *Chiasso*, or Close. Some of these too are family closes, but there are Measures Close where weighing was done, the Close with the Hole, the Close of the Armed Men—all reminders of industries vanished or of incidents nonetheless forgotten.

Then there are the Corners: Stationers' Corner, Boltmakers' Corner, Flagmakers' Corner, Orange Tree Corner, Four Lions Corner near Santo Spirito which was probably where an inn stood or had stood. Others make one speculate: Flies' Corner, Wise Man's Corner, And over one you can either chuckle or sigh: the Corner of the Need.

These small interlocking bye-ways and passages are the real heart of Florence. They have been and they are. The life in them today may not be grouped so picturesquely as these names in their time indicated, but an hour among them is not mere historical study. They are not like certain lanes in the City of London, where people work but do not live, and work in an occupation that has nothing to do with puddings or bread. Here people both work and live. And the shapes of their homes can profoundly alter their lives, as all architecture affects and alters lives, and as we will be seeing more specifically in a later chapter.

Goldsmiths may attract tourists to the Ponte Vécchio and internationally known workers in leather may have elegant if not very specious *botteghe*. But the majority of florentine craftsmen live and work in much humbler circumstances.

The small lanes and alleys are dim even in summer. Italy's brilliant sunlight stops overhead and does not descend by the cracks that separate the tall buildings. Joiners work on pavements in fine weather, because there is more air, or more light, or more room. Many craftsmen do not have even a *bottega:* they create in confined homes with a numerous family, and sell to middlemen.

Not only art workers, but blacksmiths, coppersmiths, sellers of cooking stoves, sellers of candles, broom-makers, box-makers, milk shops, cheese shops: in Florence anything that can be specialised is specialised. For fingers that have learned all there is to learn inside a restricted trade.

This is another of Florence's abundances: specialised mechanics. A motorcar that has crashed has need of many clinics, for general repair works are few. It must find a radiator specialist, a car electrician, a bodywork man, a car upholsterer, a tyre repairer, a speedometer specialist, even a carburettor specialist.

There exist all-round mechanics, as foremen in car manufacturers' agencies, one of which still bears on its portal, cut into the stone, the grand name Isotta-Fraschini, although it is years since those proud beauties of the road, world-second only to Rolls-Royce, were beaten out of the market by mass-rolled tinplate. But most prefer to set up on their own in their own trade, often in premises little bigger than a shed, with a single apprentice who may be a relative.

This distribution of craft, not limited to motorcars, is due to the Florentine's desire to go his own way. Because of it, the flood might have wrecked Florence for ever. Largely because of it also, the Flood did not. But more of this later.

Some craftsmen work underground. The most dismal (I am using the word 'craftsman', i.e. a man who has skill in his own trade, as a translation of the word *artigiani*, for which these qualify) are the ragmen. This is a recognised trade. They go round with barrows crying *'Donne-e-e! C'è 'cenciaio-*

o-o-o-o!' (Ladies! Here comes the ragman!) and collecting old clothes, stuffs, rags, motheaten mats, which they trundle back to their basements near Santa Croce. The good they sort from the bad and resell it. The hopeless they turn-in to industrialists at Prato, who have a process for re-spinning and re-weaving it into blankets and cheap cloth. In Prato too, home industries flourish; for many Prato magnates supply machinery to the spinners, who work them at home, sometimes clandestinely.

Much of old Florence lives underground like this. In the cellars of palazzi under gracious arches of *pietra serena* cooks and printers ply their crafts. The houses that line the San Lorenzo market all have basement shops of boots, jackets, boilersuits, called *sdruccioli* because the ladder-like entrances are so steep it is almost easier for customers to slither down. The little piazza called Limbo, where once was a children's cemetery[1] is well below the level of the street and even of the river bank nearby. You go into it down steps. Whether this is because in time the level of streets has been raised, or whether the buildings have sunk on what was formerly a swamp, I do not know. Maybe both.

Though Florence is flat, one must keep one's eyes on the ground. Pavements are narrow and kerbs of unequal height. Maybe for this reason Florentines walk slowly. Their women have not the proud slow self sufficient stalk that tells the roman woman. They tend to gossip in narrow passages or where signposts or chains restrict passage. So do their men. The others do not mutter or curse at their way being barred. They wait ostentatiously till the block clears or shoulder through with a quiet formal *Permesso?*[2]

Who keeps his eyes on the ground in Florence will find that the manhole covers are made in Florence. So are some in Rome.

---

[1] The souls of the unbaptised are committed to Limbo in catholic symbology.

[2] This is not true of bus stops, however, where no Richmond scrum would permit such pushing and wild heaving.

Dwellers and workers in some of these streets earn very little. Straw-workers, for instance. For putting together a bag of knitted straw, cutting out the pockets and lining, sewing all by a machine and adding a metal handle, each is paid about 1s 2d. The work takes over half an hour in speedy hands.

In these byeways are the true, unaged, fashionless Florentines of history: courteous, hospitable, dignified, modest of themselves, exaggeratedly proud of their city, its beauty and fame. For their city they demand compliments, but not for themselves. Pay a Tuscan a sincere compliment, and he thinks you are pulling his leg.

The small streets have loud voices. They bandy jokes about horns on their neighbours' heads and references to fruits of different shapes, mostly figs, at the slightest provocation. They argue, *fortissimo*, but practically: being voices of neither theologians nor theorists, they talk by facts. This makes them despise a drunk. He cannot reason, his arguments are emotions.

It has been said that Florentines are sharp to find an opponent's weak spot instinctively and to exploit it wilfully: and I agree. Luigi Ugolini[1] says he once saw, in the days of sartorial elegance of the edwardian type, a gloved dandy passing a beggar. With some reluctance the dandy put a coin in the upturned hand. Immediately a small street urchin whipped out a grubby handerchief and called: ' 'Ere Mister! Want to dry-off the sweat?'

In the small streets the Florentines stare at the strange, not at the stranger: girls in mini-skirts, the first bearded and bespectacled american sculptors, an old woman over-made-up. One abnormally tall man was embarrassed by the stare of an urchin. 'Haven't you ever seen a man as tall as me?' he demanded irritably. 'Not wivout payin'' retorted the urchin.

In the small streets there is often dismay, not often complaint. There are slums, and the suffering which makes and is made by

---

[1] A florentine artist who wrote *Firence Viva* published in Turin in 1962, when he was old.

slums. Sentimental people have called them happy slums, being taken in by the vivacity, the neighbourliness, the common life much in the open. But no slums are happy, and these are not. The weak, the over-sensitive and the timid perish in them. A carpenter with eight children was moved from a slum to a fine new worker's-dwelling. Memories, hopes so often gone bad into dreads—who knows what confluence of past despairs—convinced him that the new home could never be his. People were envious of him and would take it away from him. So he locked himself in the front room, broke up the furniture and started shooting madly out of the window at anyone in sight. He was moved again, this time to the lunatic asylum.

But for centuries the small streets have known siege, floods, wars, civil wars, occupation, slumps, poverty, starvation. The stronger know that if better is to come, they must go out their own way to bring it in themselves. They have no belief in abstract justice and little faith in organisations as organisations, even if these say they will hand out justice. Justice to them is a stone statue in one of the piazzas. It stands on a pillar from the Baths of Caracalla in Rome, too high to be seen. Its bronze cloak was added later.

One of their streets was called Justice Street, *Via della Giustizia*. Along it the condemned walked with formally penitent candles in their hands from the prison to the gallows. It is now called the *Via de' Malcontenti*.

20

Houses Under the Soil

A resident of many years in Florence can have walked a street hundreds of times and yet find something not noticed before to hold his attention: a window, a lunette, a carved head or design, even a whole palazzo.

Not all these are antique nor attached to famous names. What was evidently a *trattoría* in a style of this century may leave behind it over its nailed-up door a carving of a St Peter fish, a glass, and a litre-carafe, the kind, in green Empoli glass, that wine is served in.

Florence is full of such things. Discovering them does not make one feel an ignorant or unobservant stranger. It is more like finding a new meaning in a phrase of a poem long known and admired.

But it is chestertonianly disturbing to discover an unknown garden on the top of a known street. This happened to me.

I was passing along a minor street called *Via del Moro*, and suddenly saw tall trees, wistaria, a disused aviary, on top of the houses beside me.

Stopping at a *bottega* opposite, I asked what it was.

'A garden' said the smith.

'Whose?'

'The Niccolinis'.'

'But why on top of the houses?'

He shrugged his shoulders. 'They were coach houses. In the parallel street is now a garage.'

I remembered. I had left my car there many times. Near a

hanging festoon of loose virginia creeper, which almost tickled the pavement. I had never questioned it.

Seeing my continued astonishment, the smith shrugged his shoulders again and spread out his hands palm-upward. 'The Niccolini family made it' he said. 'Not I.'

21

High Summer

After the holm-oaks' cream of catkins has turned biscuit-coloured in may, after the chocolate of the new-ploughed soil has become grey dust, when the first bats flit over the heads of thigh-booted fishermen by the Arno weirs and round their friends lining the parapet to watch (with a golden cocker sitting at attention on top of it), Florence expects hot weather.

Expects, but may be wrong. Not a soul in Tuscany has any weatherlore. Ask a farmer, when the air is damp and martins in their circles are scraping the ground, if rain is likely tonight, and he will answer 'It might rain.' But he does not prepare for it. When a vine-grower decides to hold off the grape harvest for yet four days to make the wine perfect, he has to bet.

This lack of prescience is due in part to the unforeseeable storm-bringing summer winds. If they blow from the north, they blow damp and chilly: if from the south, they blow damp and clammy: but always a strong wind brings rain. To confuse further, Florence is in an odd meteorological spot. In winter a north wind can deposit deep snow from Murmansk to the Appennines, and start again dropping it from Lake Bolsena to Sicily, leaving the hollow of Florence as dry and firm as in april.

Tuscans accept change in weather as they accepted tyrants and archdukes: one day out, one day in: but the Tuscans went on living.

High summer is very hot. Continuous strilling of cicalas, all on one note but never monotonous, makes the heat hotter. Cypresses smell of boiling turpentine. Jackets fall off and formality dies. The stuffiest english visitor envies the american with a pyjama shirt outside his trousertops.

The unstuffy can go too far. An Englishman walked into the Duomo Square clad in sandals, shorts, crushed hat and tobacco pipe. His body was as undistinguished as he was. His face was self-absorbed. I felt myself a link of shame between Britain and Florence. The sun was not even noonday.

'Mad dogs and Englishmen.' It is true of Italy: but I am not sure how mad the Englishmen are. Certainly after a year or two of residence one leaves the pride of the sun for the ease of the shade. But when you have few hours at your disposal it is far madder to spend them sweating on a bed, if you could be moving as sweatily but slow and alone amid still architecture. Englishmen are mad only if they go out after lunch expecting to enter churches or museums, which are closed.

Mad dogs in Italy, because of muzzle-or-leash orders, and the duty of slaughterers to destroy any dog found in public without an identifying collar, are as rare as love-philtres, anyway.

Spontaneous hydrophobia in humans round Florence is even rarer. Drought is regular each year. We have been over a fortnight without a drop of water in a house containing four adults, two children and two small babies. In another house we had to fetch water from a cave we found it in. The cave was near a road, and we hid from passing motorists; else half the city would have been up and no nappies washed.

The country round-about is streaked with watercourses marked *torrenti*. Summer visitors make wry jokes about their dry beds: but in winter these are indeed torrents, foaming, gushing, galloping, tumbling, able to kill livestock and men. Plans are agreed every year or two for bigger and better reservoirs, but are disagreed the following year. The Guelphs and Ghibellines, Blacks and Whites, are at their games all over again, and reach less agreement than the Ouse Catchment Board used to do in Huntingdonshire. There by an unwritten and unspoken law as the river backed up from the Wash, each member of the Board handed it higher and higher upstream, until it reached the great meadows above St Ives. As this happened every year, the farmers of St Ives forded off their cattle in time, and the Ouse could flood to its heart's content and the full pressure of the tide at King's Lynn.

Not so here. Measures are taken to allocate by districts what water there is, to ration it fairly at night, so as to fill buckets and baths. But somehow the centre of the burden always seems to fall on Rifredi, a workers' district, to the detriment of its fish shops and of wineglass-cleaning in its bars. There is grumbling then, but more at the inevitability than at the inconvenience.

All Florentines who can, make for mountains or sea, according to the temperaments of their children. For sea air is supposed to make children nervous by the same young-wives'-tale as made edwardian mothers swither between the 'bracing' east coast of England and the 'relaxing' south coast for summer holidays.

If they can afford it, and many can (or do), the families go off without the father for two or three months, to cheap lodgings, or a rented house, or a caravan placed in a pinewood. Strips of ancient and gigantic stonepines line the tuscan coast for miles and miles. The breadwinner motors out for week-ends, and works hard on lonely hot weekdays to avoid being unfaithful. Wives do their best at the other end among new acquaintances.

Indeed it may be to avoid infidelities that so many Florentines take their summer holidays in the same place as their friends,[1] with the result that from Forte dei Marmi[2] and beyond to Viareggio and beyond, the coast is one long string of re-united Florentine families and their neighbours. Just as

---

[1] Some, perhaps, to continue their infidelities?

[2] Near Carrara, hence the name. A minor watering-place with hundreds of small houses ready to be let to, or newly built by, Florentines.

in Margate the dwellers in Hackney and Bow used to greet the same neighbours, when they took in the milk of a morning, as they greeted at home. I don't know if they still do.

Anyone who wishes to see Florence when it is almost quite empty of Florentines, should go there round about the 15th of august, the Feast of the Assumption of the Virgin Mary. This is usually called by the shorter name of *Ferragosto*, or August Fair. Justly enough, seeing that it has been going since the time of Augustus Caesar, who instituted it, and probably gave his name to the english August Bank Holiday too. Nobody who has to remain in Florence does any work. Tourists have the quiet place to themselves, and sometimes make it noisy with long-distance coaches and bad manners. For in this month, among good tourists tied for freedom dates to school calendars, there appear also bad tourists, who stay for an afternoon and a night, and do little but shriek and eat ice creams.

It was in august that a young foreigner on the Ponte Vecchio, just off a high-speed touring coach, was seen to draw a sheaf of papers from his pocket and heard to answer a group of girl fellow travellers: 'Why, this must be Florence. Today's thursday!'

Villa residents who remain through these months can be troubled by insects. Mosquitoes become really pungent. Spiders, some of which have mandibles that bite, swarm unless they are eaten by scorpions. The scorpions are small and black and not as dangerous as the dirty-yellow big ones of Spain or the South of Italy. Sometimes they pinch with their pincers before they sting with their tail: so you can be warned in time.

But scorpions do not swarm if they are eaten by scorpion-eaters. These are millipedes called *scolopendre*, crustaceans armoured in segments of shell as hard as a lobster's, with whiskered heads like a chinese dragon. They can grow up to 20 centimetres long, and should be destroyed on sight. But if

143

to destroy a scorpion requires a hammer, to destroy a *scolopendra* requires a hammer, a strong wrist, a good eye, determination, and fury. The last comes easily as a revenge for fear.[1]

Scolopendre coil on themselves like cobras, but they do not jump. They move fast, but not so fast as centipedes. These are harmless, fluffy, honey-coloured, many-legged crawlies an inch or two long according to age, which run up walls and always seem in a panic. If you hit them, they disintegrate. They only tickle.[2]

Snakes are few. An occasional viper is reported near Florence, and one or two exceptionally inside it. But it does appear that they are becoming more numerous because of the drift away from the land, which is leaving estate after estate unworked and uninhabited. I have seen in Chianti vipers as long and as thick as grass snakes. There is not much one can do about them, except to avoid them if one can, and if one can't, to keep moving and get to hospital within an hour.

On the other hand insect life provides many beautiful compensations: butterflies, moths, beetles. Gardens are vivid with butterflies all through the summer: tortoiseshells, swallowtails, admirals red and white, coppers, browns, blues, whites, green, sulphur, primrose. Humming-bird moths hover like their tropical bird namesakes at the doors of flowers, sucking out honey through long probosces. At night all kinds of moths come in: from the Hawks, including the not uncommon Death's-Head, to the Goat, the Puss, Tigers and Wainscots. Beetles, that scare some adults, delight children. There is a big one which looks like a black rhinoceros; there is the *cerambyx* with antennae longer than its back, who is never far from his mate and seems to die when the mate dies. There are praying-

---

[1] A scientific account credits these beasts with four eyes each. I must confess that my own have never lingered long enough on them to notice this.

[2] It is possible that I have got my terms mixed, and a centipede is a millipede and *vice versa*. But chilopods and hexapods (should they not be hecatopods?) are a branch of natural history I do not care to pore over, even in illustrations.

mantis, slow, green, mystical. One mantis bit me once. It felt like two bits of cardboard clenching my finger not breaking the skin, as firm and blunt and in a way gentle as the bite of Peggy, the pygmy hippopotamus who was once my friend in the London Zoo.

There are wasps and honey bees, bumble bees and flies of all sizes and colours. There are the sweet pale green and blue and translucent damsel flies we get in Britain. There are grasshoppers, crickets, locusts and hornets. Little wall lizards, some scarcely larger than newts, wriggle nervously into walls, under stones, behind a leaf which trembles. In the angle of a door may wait a gecko, ugly but friendly, which to the horror of newcomers tuscan folk call a 'tarantula.' At night the little scops owl calls 'kyu-u' in a regular rhythm of mournfulness like the foghorn of a falsetto lighthouse. The nightingales have gone, or are too busy packing to sing.

This is the season of peaches, and if you buy a yellow not a green one off a barrow, you should stoop forward or its bursting syrup will stain your front. It is the season of apricots still, of figs, of melons. On a hot night all over the city people stop to buy whangs of water-melon, cool dark green outside like night in a norwegian forest, and wet fresh red inside like a wine past its best. Many a supper in a villa garden or on the starlit terrazza of a flat ends with a whole one, for the chilling of which the fridge has been evacuated.

Now landscapes which at summer's beginning were so clear that distant hills seemed magnified under water, are hazed over with heat like mildew on a picture. Fields that have been yellow with hawkbit and corn marigold are levelled down. Their fringes are white now not with iris but with umbrellas of hemlock, skated on by spotty burnets. Church bells travel and echo: the deep boom of the Duomo like Tom of Christchurch's over Oxford, the clash of San Lorenzo's peal worthy of Boulez, the tinkle of convent bells nearer by, behind high walls, each with its own voice and rhythm, of which one performs the opening bars of the *Golliwog's Cake-walk*,[1] they seem to hang longer in the air than at other seasons.

Hoopoes still leap from tree to tree, but in silence. Under a pine branch a yellow-green oriole sits without moving, also in silence. The scent of wild fennel by the roadside is close and aromatic. A grasshopper zizzles.

This is lazy weather. One is tempted to do nothing. Not move, not read, not listen, not talk, not sleep. Enough to be.

But to be is to be others. These hours are not lost. Not thinking, not dreaming, one absorbs. One belongs. In the solitude other people percolate into one. People one is made of. Florentine people.

Watch in the breeze the hopeful gestures of cypress-tips like those of helpless and rooted puppets.

If there is a breeze.

Up there.

[1] Piano-piece by Debussy popular even in my youth among fellow-students who thought this composer ultra-modern.

22

Panache of a Beggar

A young couple are sitting at a table in a roofed-in courtyard near the Pitti Palace. They are eating the best *pizza*[1] north of Rome and possibly the best north of Naples. So the girl says.

One is eating a neapolitan *pizza* covered with cheese and origanum and tomato and anchovies, the other a *Pizza of the Four Seasons*, where you pick your taste from each of its four quarters. In this *pizzería* the pastry fills an entire big plate.

People pass through the courtyard, which is a public short cut through an area blown up by the Germans needlessly in their last retreat.

A badly dressed man leaves the stream of passers by and asks the young man very politely, 'Have you a hundred lire, please?'

Astonished, because he doesn't know him, the young man produces the coin.

'Thank you' says the badly-dressed man, and quietly goes away.

The young man and the young woman stare at each other.

---

[1] *Pizza* should never be called Pizza Pie. It is not a pie, which has been a covered dish since Middle English times. It might be a tart, but is never made with fruit. It is between pastry and unleavened bread, and for perfection requires an oven so hot that italian housewives, when they make it, often prefer to take it to the baker's to be fired.

23

A Very Brief History of the Florentine Theatre

The great pioneer painter Cenni di Pepo, who was so truculent in a city of truculent men that they called him 'Poll-the-Ox' (*Cimabue*), might very well never have achieved his breakaway from mediaeval byzantine abstractions if the semi-dramatic *làude* had never come to Florence.

Not that the byzantine church did not have its liturgical dramas: a dialogue between the Virgin Mary and the Angel of the Annunciation derives from the time if not the pen of a Patriarch of Constantinople in the seventh century. But byzantine painters did not take their chance.

The *làudesi* were not Florentines. They came over the border from Umbria. They were groups of flagellants, extreme followers of St Francis, who would probably have deplored their penitential excesses. They flogged each other while singing antiphons to the glory of God. They set out from Assisi and Perugia and wandered Europe doing so. They started european drama.

St Francis had not been long dead and into their 'lauds' they inserted his Canticle of Brother Sun. Chanting other reasons for praising God, they began to impersonate saints and prophets whose deeds or words they were extolling. A kind of embryonic drama, not unlike that of Thespis[1], started in

---

[1] Sixth century B C. The first greek actor and dramatist we know of. He seems to have had a car or cart: but whether he toured or merely carried his costumes and masks in it, is not yet certain.

148

churches when the platform or thalamus they chanted from was backed by a painted Mount. Dramatic locality was born.

The Mount could open to disclose the Nativity or to let the Saviour descend into Limbo. It could serve as the Mount of Olives or for the Crucifixion. When they took this out and chanted below the Tabernacles of the Virgin in the city, the street changed its locality and bystanders changed their nature. They entered another locality as audience. The street became a theatre.

Because the church was passing through, or into, a sumptuous phase, St Francis or no, flagellants or no, these actors gathered a sumptuous wardrobe. Costume was born. But at the same time they were essentially people of their own period. Many of their mimed songs were in the form of minstrels' ballads. Thus one *làuda* to the Virgin began *Rayna potentissima sopra el cel seti assaltata* which I am assured on good authority is pure minstrels' metre.

According to Piero Bargellini[1] some florentine painters actually helped them with their Mount, and in time, with other scenery: and of these young Poll-the-Ox may have been one. According to Bargellini he certainly found on the Mount stage that human figures need not be encased in their own features and isolated with gold-leaf. On the contrary, they were better when open to the air, the place, the other people, and the time: to their locality, in fact. And this surround composed them.

'The very same colour' says Bargellini, 'which in the figure of a byzantine saint has the same intensity from head to foot, on the Mount created *chiaroscuro* varying from crest to shoulders, from flank to level ground.' Would abstract art today, I wonder, make other new discoveries if it allied itself to some movement outside pictorial art?

That was in the mid-thirteenth century. Within forty or

---

[1] *Vedere e Capire Firenze* (Florence 1958). For later references to him as a man see the Index.

fifty years Florence was leading Italy in religious plays, written for a lay public in their own language, and performed in the Piazza della Signoría, the new square.

In all there were more than a hundred of them. Usually they were connected with civic processions on Saints' or other feast days, such as at Easter. The stages were on wheels. They could even be on boats. In 1306 there was a show of *Heaven and Hell* on the Arno. Something from that lingers yet, perhaps, in the Feast of the Rificolone, when the nights are drawing in, and children carry chinese lanterns on sticks to the Arno where illuminated boats ply up and down.

The great event of the public year in Florence, however, was the feast on the 24th of june in honour of John the Baptist, the city's patron saint. On such a day in the following century an epic show from the *Fall of Lucifer* to the *Last Judgment* lasted sixteen hours. Today there are no more *sacre rappresentazioni*. There are fireworks instead. The Brownings saw them as they floated down the Arno in a boat, for at that time the fireworks were launched on the Ponte alla Carraia (not unsuitably: the Feast of John the Baptist was superimposed on the pagan Midsummer Festival of Water). Nowadays they come from the Piazzale Michelangelo. Visible from Settignano almost to Sesto Fiorentino, the sky explodes. The costly spectacle is planned in rhythms, *crescendo ed accelerando*, to an uninterrupted finale: after which there is a second's pause and a bang like a broken sound barrier. Double, too, with the echo off the hills.

These people's-dramas continued under the Medicis. Lorenzo, who was himself a notable singer and composer of impromptu songs in the popular idiom, fitted his own words to popular tunes for carneval scenes, triumphs, cars, and masques for the delectation (and perhaps unification) of lords and people. In 1489 he created *St John and St Paul*, an expression of his political ethic. It was also earthy in words and humour. Such earthiness remained part of more elevated themes in all countries: even the folk-lore bridal plays of the mummers in

Greece and in England contained what were later thought obscenities and were suppressed by moustachioed policemen or victorian parsons. In Florence it goes on in popular song and sketch, and particularly in the *stornello*.

This is a sung dialogue in its true form, the words impromptu, the best of the tunes hauntingly melodic and often allowing for a kind of *flamenco* on a single vowel to give the singer time to think out the next line. Allusions are made, in mock innocence, to the usual fruits.

It lived long as an also upper-class diversion in Florence. In 1765–6, when theatres were closed at the death of the Emperor Francis I, who was also Duke of Tuscany, the *stornello* helped to replace opera and drama in the Pergola and Cocomero Theatres. Even in the nineteenth century the middle classes attended evenings of it. And today there is a public competition held each autumn at the Porta Romana during a popular feast called the Feast of the Birds, which is not mentioned in guide books. As well as in *stornelli*, contadini and others compete in whistled imitations of birdsong, many of them being old men in sharp falsetto.

I would hesitate to trace the *stornello* directly back to the *làuda*. But this bears thinking about.

To return to court entertainments. In all, Lorenzo is said to have staged fifteen 'triumphs' of this sort, which were performed by a group called the Company of the Star. It seems to have been professional, or semi-professional.

The idea of a *mascherata* not as a mere romp but as a calculated dramatic event, and especially the adoption of the mask or vizor in character, gave a lead here in Florence to what would become the delight and fame of the Tudor court revels in England, where it arrived at Epiphany 1513 for the first time, thanks to the leader of England's Renaissance, the handsome and artistic twenty-two-year-old King Henry VIII.

Popular shows continued through the sixteenth century, culminating in a consciously artistic work called *Adam* in 1613, written by Giambattista Andreini, one of a family of professional actors who was born in Florence in 1578.

Apart from this, the lead in the new and more serious drama (tragedy, comedy, pastoral in imitations of the Classics), passed to Mantua, Padua, Venice and Ferrara, with authors like Tasso and Ariosto. Florence was too preoccupied in trying to restore its lost democracy, now dictated over by popes, now by emperors. Both these sources of power in the end created a Duke of Florence, later promoted to Grand Duke. He came from Medici stock, but the direct line had died out.

Under him and his brother Ferdinand the arts were not neglected: for names, there were Cellini, Bronzino, Buontalenti, the mannerist painters. The baroque period set in. As an architectural style, however, baroque did not suit the sober, balanced florentine spirit. The writhing glory of baroque lies mainly in its technique, by which stone seems to be silk or velvet, and a Madonna's head seems to eclipse a star of flaming gold. Flat ceilings inflate themselves to great heights, so that over craned human necks below the under-soles of human feet seem to stand on solid air. But the spiritual result of this is very near hallucination,[1] and Florentines liked neither drunk men nor drunk buildings.

Baroque churches tend to become baroque statues, and baroque statues seem full of water pressure, about to become fountains. Florence has few fountains, material or psychic. Founded on water, she has little in common with water. Despite the Boboli Gardens and the Grand Duke in the Pitti Palace, she refused to follow Bernini.

Baroque theatre she thus missed altogether. She turned instead to theatrical music. The idea matured in the *Camerata de' Bardi*.

The Bardi had been a merchant banker family like the Medicis, but in the thirteenth century much richer. They made

---

[1] Which may account for its growing popularity in these mescalin days.

the mistake of financing King Edward III of England at the beginning of the Hundred Years' War. They went bankrupt in 1345, the year before the Battle of Crecy. In the course of time they grew rich again, but never to the measure of the Medicis (their coat of arms bore three balls instead of six); and powerful enough to be given the title of Counts of Vernio.

Count Giovanni had his palazzo not in the Via de' Bardi[1] for the old one had been destroyed, but between Piazza Santa Croce and the bridge over the Arno called the Ponte alle Grazie, after a Madonna which then surmounted it. This palazzo is said to have been designed by Brunelleschi. It is still there, shored up on one side because of the Flood of 1966.

Count Giovanni was a good musician, and gathered round him others, as good musicians do, to play and compose what we would call chamber music. Florence was a home of music. Her church organs were famous. So were Squarcialupi, organist in the Duomo from 1450 on, who was also lutanist and singer; and Maestro Antonio di Guido for his improvised serious songs.

The musicians of the Camerata were mostly nobles. There was old Vincenzo Galilei, father of the astronomer, who wrote a Dialogue on Ancient and Modern Music; there was Laura Guidiccini, an accomplished lady of the Lucchesini family: there was one of the Strozzis. Others were serious musicians who do not seem to have been nobles. Their professed interest was in the music used, or supposed to have been used, in classical greek theatres. It seemed to them, on somewhat flimsy evidence, that the solo voice accompanied by simple instruments which did not take part in, or take over, the melody could be preferable as music to the interwoven polyphony in vogue in churches, and even preferable to what Francis Bacon called the 'Broken Music or Consort Music' of

---

[1] Part of the action in George Eliot's *Romola* is placed in this.

halls and gardens. That is to say, preferable to the vocal and instrumental music heard all round them.

If their beliefs had prevailed universally, there would have been no chamber music as we know it; no Bach, Mozart, Beethoven, Brahms or Alban Berg.

Basing himself on old Galilei, Giulio Caccini[1] experimented in writing 'monody,' to be accompanied by Bardilla, a well-known professional, on the theorbo. The theorbo was an enlarged or augmented lute with a wide compass, capable of sturdy and almost orchestral chords. He and Jacopo Corsi found it better to leave the composing of this accompaniment to the musical intuitions of whoever was playing theorbo or harpsichord (another instrument capable of strong chords). For this purpose one or both of them invented the 'figured bass' for *continuo* which Bach used and others much later.

In their deliberate search for the antique, this group had taken a step backward into popular music. But, as some backward steps sometimes do, this altered perspective, and opened new horizons. *Recitativo*, for instance. Free singing, accompanied by lumps of instrumental sound, need not be limited to lyrics set in four-square melody: it could also sing prose speech.

The next step on this line was to wed music with theatre and beget Opera.

There was a poetical dramatist called Ottavio Rinuccini who frequented the Camerata. He was a friend of Maria de' Medici and often visited her at the court of France after she married Henri IV. Whatever was in the florentine air thus passed to Paris.

He wrote a play called *Dafne* to which the new music was written by the Maestro di Cappella of the Grand Dukes, Jacopo Peri,[2] a long-haired dishevelled little figure who was known as *Il Zazzerino* (Little Shock-head). Count Giovanni by this time had gone to Rome as Maestro di Camera to Pope

---

[1] 1560–1618   [2] 1561–1633

Clement VII. So the first performance of the first opera in the world[1] took place in the Palazzo of the Corsi family in 1597 during Carneval, with Peri himself singing Apollo.

This is the Palazzo in the Via Tornabuoni, almost opposite the 'English Chemist's,' which the Corsi family had bought in the previous century. A small theatre was fitted up for the purpose; but the building was much altered in 1864 when the Via Tornabuoni was widened.

Three years later the same poet and composer presented a *Eurydice*, commissioned for performance on 9 february 1600 at the wedding of Maria de' Medici. As this was an immensely important court function, I take it to have been produced either in the forty-year-old courtyard of the Pitti Palace, where concerts are still given, or more likely in the amphitheatre in the gardens, which was used for court functions and is still used for open-air opera.

It is strange that from this un-baroque, indeed anti-baroque, city should have sprung italian opera and oratorio, more florid than any other baroque music. It is strange that the Theatre of the Pergola should have given its form to opera houses all over Europe and even South America. But having made this contribution, Florence retired from creative theatre.

Rinuccini lived for another twenty years but seems to have done nothing more. Peri lived for thirty-three. He went to Mantua, where Monteverdi transplanted the new art form and gave it everlasting fruit. Indeed Peri and Monteverdi collaborated there in an *Arianna* in 1608, Peri as the expert writing the *recitativi* and the six-year younger Monteverdi surrounding the *arias* with his new-fangled unresolved discords which were to rouse opposition for years.[2]

The new form spread. Giulio Caccini composed a *Eurydice*

---

[1] Or, in Europe, if you care to call the dramas that have been going in China since the thirteenth century by the name of operas.

[2] Harmonically, in our now long historical perspective Monteverdi's *Orfeo* in 1608 has something in common with Berg's *Wozzek* in 1922.

to challenge Monteverdi's: Filippo Vitali with his *Aretusa* in a private palace in 1620 converted Rome to it. Opera was airborne. But so far as Florence is concerned, despite the presence of Alessandro Scarlatti the Southerner, who composed operas for the private theatre of Ferdinand III of Tuscany, there her short story ends.

By the eighteenth century opera in Florence, as elsewhere, had become a social occasion, and doomed to remain so till the first world war. However delicate the arias on the stage, the audience continuously got up and moved about visiting each other, chatting loudly and laughing. At one time they used to have suppers served in the boxes. If later these became ices in summer and sweets in winter, it was not from respect for the show, but because the audience had already eaten at home. Perhaps they were right in their inattention. Real horse-chariots and real camels on the stage have little to do with music.

Only the ballet held their attention: and according to the Earl of Cork and Orrery, the performance of this was dismal. No graceful postures, charming turns, light steps. The women whirled clumsily, the men merely jumped as high as possible— exactly what this noble critic had complained of in London.

But Florence was mad about ballet. All classes and professions. Many monasteries and nunneries had their private dance theatres, where in the one case some nuns were cast as men and in the other monks as women. This explains the very few little theatres which still exist inside ecclesiastical houses here: though I doubt if dainty revels are still held in them, for the modern public to be excluded from.

Seasons of opera and drama were begun in Florence by a group of young courtiers stimulated by the Grand Duke's son, another Lorenzo de' Medici. When he died in 1648 this group called itself the *Accademia degli Immobili*, or Immobiles' Club to present and direct them. Its crest was a Windmill ('In Its Motion It Stands Still'): and it built a small theatre called the

156

Watermelon in 1652 in the street of that name (*Cocomero*) which was changed in 1859 to Ricasoli Street.

This theatre was found to be too narrow, so in the very same year the club built a bigger one in the Street of the Pergola. But some members stayed at the Watermelon, as a breakaway or rather staybehind fraction, which they called the *Accademia degli Infuocati*. This means not the Burnt Generation, but 'Made Ardent.' The Watermelon, later named the Niccolini Theatre after the poetic dramatist of the mid-nineteenth century, is now a cinema. The odd ball carved over the door-way is not a sprouting water-melon but a kind of flaming grenade, badge of what made them ardent.

For ardent Scots it may be added in parentheses that among the many distinguished people who attended the Pergola Theatre the Young Pretender was often seen, both before the '45 and in his later alcoholic years with his horrible and faithless wife.

Straight drama was also given, but its standard was little better than that of the ballet. The Earl of Cork longed for the good sense, naturalness and dignity of action and dialogue and the elegant scenery of the London stage. But, as I have quoted elsewhere, Riccaboni, who travelled Europe in the eighteenth century found the naturalness of english actors preferable to the stage art of any other european country, years before Garrick.

On the other hand the Earl loved the lay-out of the Pergola. Its shape was preferable to any other theatre's that he knew, more harmonious and agreeable than even his beloved Hay-market.

In the season 1743–4 a professional impresario was hired to direct shows: the standard seems to have dropped further. But musical standards were always higher than dramatic. By 1775 the orchestra was led by Nardini, Head of the Violin School of Tuscany and composer of works still played by virtuosi.

Meantime other groups were opening theatres. One was for amateur opera singers: the Piazza Vecchia Theatre, altered from an inn called The Eagle, by the Venturesomes' Club (*Accademia degli Arrischiati*). In the same year 1766, a theatre in what is now the Via Ghibellina (but previously known prophetically,[1] since it was one of the worst hit in the 1966 flood, as the Street of the Waters) had been built by lay brothers called the *Confraternita di San Paolo*. This was leased to the Young Eagles' Club. Also in the same year the old Meruzzi Palace in Borgo dei Greci was disposed-of for concerts and improvised songs, to be known as the Santa Maria Teresa. The club which ran this was called the Harmonics', and was later replaced by the *Cadenti*. I have no idea why: this word for 'dropping' implied sleep, debility or old age. It may have been defiant-ironic. But all this gives some idea of the social movements of the time, which presumably had some effects on choice and treatment of productions.

Most of these premises could be used for other purposes: masked balls at carneval, gambling (basset or faro), even horse shows. Next year the Grand Duke called a halt. Something like the London Patent Theatres were instituted.

All shows must have granducal approval before production, in imitation of what had been done by the Pope in Rome ten years before. The Pergola was given the monopoly of opera during carneval, but had to supply at least two shows of six performances each. The Watermelon was free to open all the year, but with straight drama only during carneval and in the autumn—and with musical burlesques in spring, provided that at least two 'books' had at least fifteen performances each. The Santa Maria and Piazza Vecchia Theatres could give straight drama and carneval balls. All other theatres were closed.

In 1808 however the court itself pulled down the sad convent of Annalena near the Pitti Palace, and built a beautiful small

---

[1] Or retrospectively, perhaps?

theatre, seating about 800, which was connected with the
Palace by an underground walk. This within living memory
has been used for children's shows, but stands alas! tattered
and battered by war and post-war uses. Its stage is enormous,
and fourteen decent-sized dressingrooms on it hardly reduce
the acting area. It is now called the *Teatro Goldoni* and is
used only by orchestras rehearsing for Amici della Musica
concerts.

Other buildings remained. One which had been built by
the Coletti family was sold to the 'Resolutes' Club,' then
rebuilt in 1828 as the Alfieri Theatre; which was where the
middle-classes regaled themselves with *stornelli*. This seated
1,700. It also is now a cinema. The Piazza Vecchia, on the other
hand, was pulled down by Prince Carrega to build his big
palace, which is now the Baglioni Hotel.

The Pergola was rebuilt in brick in 1739, and again rebuilt in
1837. Other nineteenth century theatres have been destroyed
only recently: the Laura for example. The Teatro delle Loggie,
near Piazza San Firenze, built in 1868, was renamed after the
great florentine actor Tommaso Salvini. The loggia which
gave it its first name is still there.

Tommaso Salvini, a kind of Joachim among actors,[1] really
belonged to all Italy. So did his grandson Guido, one of the
best producers of inter-war Italy, who broke his heart and his
fortune trying more than once to forge a national theatre.[2]
But though he lived in the family villa above Florence and
worked in a study filled with properties and prompt books
of his august ancestor, he was always going away to other
cities and other countries to produce.

Florence was not unaware of him. She invited him to
produce Shakespeare in the Boboli Gardens, when he was
technical dramatic expert to the beginnings of the Maggio

[1] Joseph Joachim (1831–1907) was a hungarian violinist who with Brahms and
others introduced a new sincerity into nineteenth century music.
[2] For an account of Guido Salvini in some detail see the present writer's article in
Theatre Research (*Récherches Théâtrales*) 1966 Vol VII no. 3.

Musicale. (He was one of the best all-round stage technicians in the world: musician, scene-designer, master of stage effects and of lighting). It was characteristic of him to decline, and to suggest instead a visit from Reinhardt (so that he could learn from him, he said privately). The result was the celebrated *Midsummer Night's Dream.* Reinhardt came to choose the site, having been provided with a revolving stage model which had been constructed to tempt him into undertaking the production. He disregarded it, paced the Boboli Gardens, and stopped unexpectedly at the Hill of the Pegasus. 'Here!' he said. 'And I will need scores of fireflies.'

The stage manager spent hours in training little men to wave electric sticks behind bushes. They were not required. On the opening night the acting area bounced, swam and signalled with real fireflies.

As Guido Salvini had asked in the same summer Jacques Copeau from Paris to produce a play about Sant'Uliva in the Santa Croce cloisters and was assistant producer to both masters, his days were spent in taking taxis from rehearsal to rehearsal.

There have been many other famous productions in the Boboli Gardens: Tasso's *Aminta,* the two existing acts of Pirandello's *Mountain Giants, Troilus & Cressida, the Tempest,* Weber's *Oberon* among them, to say nothing of ballets. But these have usually been guest or special productions for the tourist season. Florence in herself is not a theatrical city.

She accepts visits from interesting companies, like the Dublin Gate, Renzo Ricci's (the Felix Aylmer of Italy), and so on. The auditorium for these is full, but there is little financial stimulus to put on a show, so many free tickets have to be given away to the families of bigwigs and other privileged persons.

In 1908 Gordon Craig settled in Florence, where he edited *The Mask,* a periodical crammed with knowledge of theatre art all over the world and over history, intended to stimulate his time toward the new and real theatre of the arts to which he devoted his life and which the world rejected. He had organised a theatre school in the Arena Goldoni, an open space a few yards away from the Granducal Teatro Goldoni and not far from (confusingly) a modern cinema called the Cinema Goldoni, when the first world war broke out, and the project collapsed.

Florence now has a permanent tiny theatre which houses a repertory company sometimes joined by non-florentine stars. But this does not create a florentine theatre. She has one or two small local companies, who put on comedies about Florence. But these are mostly old-style in conception and livingroom-set in execution.

A few years ago an american woman playwright and ex-actress, together with a british playwright and ex-producer with his wife, all being residents, tried to organise an international theatre in english in Florence, first for summer tourists, who complain of the lack of entertainment in the evenings, then to be permanent throughout the year.

They had at their disposal, rent-free or almost, both the roman theatre at Fiesole and the disused Granducal Theatre with its underground passage from the Pitti Palace, the granducal chair still in the granducal box near the granducal fireplace: for alternative outdoor or indoor shows. They held two annual international drama competitions, one won by a british, the other by an american, playwright. For three years they laboured against the disinterest, doubts, and even insults of rich people in London, the USA and Florence, to whom they applied for the tiny sum they needed to start.

As a result of a personal visit to Rome they received a promise from the Ministry of Spectacle and Tourism, that they would be granted the balance between what they had culled and what they needed. The producer went to London, chose a talented and eager young company, and started the first reading of the opening play. A telegram arrived informing him that the sum from Rome would be not the L.6,000,000 promised, but L.250,000. The company had to be disbanded.

On this occasion it was not only the Central Government that let Florence down, but Florence itself also. The idea had been to stylise production enough that even non-english speakers could follow the drift and enjoy the dialogue. Based, of course, on the 'experimental' period of the 1920s and 1930s, which in their turn could not have happened but for Gordon Craig. Those experimental theatres disappeared because there was as yet no need for them. Here there was need. And a ready audience. Many Florentines learn english, and these and others were enthusiastic. But not Florence as such. When, recently, the Living Theatre appeared here with something of the same approach, though different in execution, the only place it could find was a club hall far from the centre, seating only a few hundreds. And the audience was mostly young.

The youth of that audience, and its positive reactions to that show may mean that theatrical winds will change, or perhaps that there will be a theatrical wind in Florence.

I set my thumb and hold it up. As yet there is no cool direction breathing on it.

24

The Car of Thespis

In an open space off a side street a marquee went up. The *guitti*, the strolling players, had arrived. Nobody expected them, nobody wanted them, and nobody much went on the opening night. People preferred to watch television.

On the poster outside the marquee, which was the only publicity, it was announced that on thursday night a television set would operate during the interval. On thursdays at that time *Lascia o Raddoppia* (Double or Quits), a parlour quiz in which amateur experts on Dante, or American History, or Famous Racehorses or any other pet subject, won large sums or lost all, held millions of heads fixed throughout Italy. The first act came to its end smoothly and punctually for Double or Quits to take over.

The poster announced that, next tuesday night, ladies would be admitted at a reduced price if accompanied by a gentleman. Seats cost 2s 6d or 1s 9d.

The poster announced that children would be admitted free. Few children went.

The poster announced that next friday night gentlemen would be admitted at a reduced price if accompanied by ladies.

Ladies and gentlemen went. They went again.

The television set disappeared.

By the end of that week ladies and gentlemen had to go early to get in.

The Car of Thespis Company[1] had come for a fortnight in

---

[1] It is possible that there is more than one company in Italy with this name, which may be generic.

march: it stayed for two and a half months. At the end of each show the audience was invited to choose a play from the repertoire, lists of which hung round the canvas walls. There were fifty plays in it, ranging from *La Dame aux Camellias* to *The Miracles of Santa Rita* (Saint of Impossibilities) 'with five real miracles on the stage.' It included the italian title of *The Eagle With Two Heads*, which is applied to one play by Jean Cocteau and another by Jean Marais.

The acting was sincere and convincing, if not all on the same level. There was no hamming and no mumbling. The leading lady had no mean talent, and Dumas Fils' hackneyed death-scene moved at least two experienced theatre-goers to tears.

Every evening there was an afterpiece, presented (in the strict sense of that abused word) with grace and humour, with impeccable timing of dialogue almost improvised.

Every morning the company was seen in the local shops buying bread and ham and vegetables.

In the evenings *Marguérite* was in the box-office and *Armand* showed the audience to their seats.

The Car of Thespis went as it had come. It left a gap.

25 ❀

Eyewitness of the Pact of Twinship

'I was there on friday the 28th of may 1965. A new and rare word: *gemellaggio*, twinship. Twinship between two cities.

'They have so much in common, you know. First, population: half a million each, more or less. Then there's Florence's time-and-land-mark, the *Duomo*. Well, Edinburgh's a Cathedral City too: she has two cathedrals, if not three.[1] Both are garrison towns. Both have universities, the one's founded in 1349, the other's in 1582: and people, you know, flock from far to consult doctors and surgeons of both, while legal cases are argued as learned, keen and crafty in the Courts of Justice here as in the Courts of Session there.

'The two have famous football teams. Each has given the world styles of domestic architecture, that are its pride still and the pleasure of visitors. If Edinburgh has its International Festival, Florence has its Maggio Musicale, which starts in may but trickles through other months with operas and concerts. Both have been national capitals, though neither always, and Florence for only a few years a century ago.

'The heart of Edinburgh is lifted to the sky on a cushion visible for miles round; the heart of Florence lies in her own breast wrapped by hills, cypresses and olives. But as the one remains the heart of Scotland, so the other remains the heart of

---

[1] The Episcopal Cathedral, the Catholic Cathedral, and St Giles's Church, which with the exception of a brief period under Charles II has not been a cathedral since John Knox said not.

Tuscany; and very high indeed stand both among the favourite cities of the world.

'I was there, in the *Hall of the Lilies* in the Signoría. A noble room. Lined with gilt fleur-de-lys on dark blue walls. The ceiling most lofty, beamed, and elaborately carved by Giuliano da Maiano, whose brother Benedetto made the famous doorway in one wall.

'It was in front of this doorway that the Pact of Twinship was signed on twin illuminated sheepskin parchments at a long antique table with tall chairs upholstered in red, dark red. In the body of the Hall I recognised most of the scottish residents in Florence. The British Consul was there, of course: and he too is a Scot, one of the Queen's Archers, as a matter of fact. I saw representatives of various sides of Florence, such as the Cardinal Archbishop, officers of the Army and Air Force, the modern composer Dallapiccola (don't know if you're familiar with his kind of music: dodecaphonic, they call it, very modern, but quite interesting, really, you know) and Emilio Pucci, whom you'll already have met.

'The Edinburgh Delegation was headed by Lord Provost Weatherstone and the Lady Provost, and by the City Officer Mr Thomson, whose uniform excited curiosity and admiration among our florentine friends. So did his personality when they met him.

'Florence's Lord Provost, or *sindaco*, wasn't any more La Pira, that fantastic little Christian dynamo, who for so long geared up the *giunta* of Florence to international politics by letters and telegrams and even personal visits to Heads of States all over the place. He'd had a long reign: but the *giunta* and the city got tired of his saintly (or was it, or was it macchiavellian?) at any rate unauthorised and often embarrassing behaviour,[1] and moved to the Left. The *Sindaco* who signed

---

[1] It is said that La Pira once saw a poor man in the street trembling with cold, took off his overcoat, flung it round the man, and continued going to his appointment as if nothing had happened.

the Pact is a communist, Lelio Lagorio, an able lawyer. Quite a young man, he is, with a face that makes you like and respect him on sight. A lot of communism here, you know. Half the farmers vote for it, perhaps most of them. But communism in Florence doesn't seem quite like Communism elsewhere. And in any case, shiftings of party politics, you might say, little affect general municipal policy. But that's another story, as Kipling said.

'At friday's ceremony Logorio wore a horizontal tricolor sash round his waist, such as every *sindaco* in the country has to wear on official occasions, even a civil wedding. Brings in the national sentiment. Not all of them have the right figure for it, and sometimes it looks undignified, even comic. Not so with Logorio. It suited him. Or he suited it, as you say in Scotland, don't you?

'However I thought the Lord Provost beat him to it sartorially. He must have a very good tailor. And that truly magnificent chain of office, everyone here was talking about it. Italians don't have such things. You'ld have expected it to be the other way round, wouldn't you?

'But the ceremony was picturesque. Much more so than anything of the kind in Britain. Outside, the door of the Hall was guarded by two stalwart and helmeted halberdiers in Florence's colours of red and white. Inside, near the table, waited three mace-bearers and three trumpeters, all in parti-coloured red and white, wearing those floppy red caps with a flap falling over the right shoulder, which you see in some of the Old Masters. They have done so since the time of the Old Masters, as a matter of fact.

'Their faces too came off of canvases of Old Masters, especially the seventh man, who carried the banner of Florence, a big red fleur-de-lys on a white ground.

'You know the history of this? The fleur-de-lys has been the symbol of Florence since nobody knows when. It's pro-bably the white or tinted iris you'll have noticed on every field edge round about. Though, if that's the case, nobody can explain how it came to be also the emblem of the French Kings in the Middle Ages. On that point, I've heard that originally ours here was not a red *flower-de-luce* (as Shakespeare called it) on a white ground but a white one on a red, until Florence was oppressed by France and changed the colours round. But this I can't quite believe, because the french standard bore yellow flowers, 'or' as the heralds say, on a dark blue ground, '*a field azure.*' And I dare hazard that the golden and blue of this hall echoes Florence's old original flag. But I'm no expert.

'The trumpeters blow a sennet or flourish or fanfare or whatever you call it before and after all ceremonies at which the *Sindaco* appears officially. When the trumpet shall sound, we shall all be ready for a speech.

'When they blow it in the open, you can hear the silver notes half across the city. But in a hall they blow temperately, discreetly, not to deafen. Florentines are not Neapolitans: they seldom exaggerate.

'I was most favourably impressed by Lagorio, whom I hadn't heard speak before. He hadn't been *sindaco* long; and wasn't much longer. But the way he read his speech! No party ranting. No pompous pauses. No rhetorical phrases. None of those calculated modulations—though of course italian is always shaped more melodiously than english, don't you think?

'He was quite simple. He didn't go back to ancient history to account for his admiration of Edinburgh, though he did compare the two cities' long fight for self-protection and freedom. With special praise to Sir Walter Scott for his influence on Manzoni (not that Manzoni had any connection with Florence that I know of).

'No, what appealed most to him was the liberal spirit of Edinburgh at the turn of the eighteenth century, more or less when the first modern literary magazine was given to the world. And it was chiefly of the present and the future that he spoke. He said both cities faced similar problems and could learn from each other, particularly as he put it, 'harmonising an ancient, splendid, untouchable city with a new and modern one, which in the future could reach out its arms in courage and pride toward the old city.'[1] I liked that.

'This was a practical, realistic speech, and was taken up at once by the Lord Provost of Edinburgh in a manner I found urgent and exciting. Not that he, either, indulged in oratory. In fact when he first came to the table, he kicked off with a quiet joke before the match began, so to speak. A simple joke, but agreeable. Scotland's leading export, you know. He put us all at our ease: the Scots among us knowing our international reputation, and the rest believing it. Looking down at the glasses and bottle of mineral water on the table, he said quite quietly, almost in a murmur: 'It's the wrong stuff.'

'Now he spoke to us with the assurance, and I thought, vision, of an able company chairman addressing the shareholders. He said the two cities had been working on this Pact for two years (so some credit ought to go to little La Pira)—he didn't say that last bit, it wouldn't have been tactful.—He quoted this year as being the one in which Florence is celebrating quater-centenaries of Michelangelo and Galileo, and the seventh centenary of Dante, all at once. He described the italian companies and artists who have contributed to the Edinburgh Festival. He offered the Scottish National Orchestra and the Opera Company to the Maggio Musicale. He too paid more attention to the future, and to an immediate and definite future at that! And very crisply and positively. Something had to be done at once, he said; and the first thing was to invite a florentine delegation to the Edinburgh Festival that coming august. That would be the first step.

'But scots education officers, he said, must come to Florence

---

[1] It is not inconceivable that the asymmetry of the Signoría may in the reader's lifetime reach out its arms to contemporary buildings, but only after much opposition has been overcome.

to see how Florence was dealing with problems that were Edinburgh's too. And not only officers, but professors, and school teachers and school children. And not only they, but housewives and mothers. Not to stay in the Grand Hotel ('Very nice indeed, the Grand Hotel!') but with other housewives and mothers. And all this to be arranged at once. 'This ceremony' he said 'will be absolutely meaningless, unless we build on it, and progress to a real interchange of people.'

'Then the parchments were signed. *Florence and Edinburgh, cities united in the affinities of their position in history, culture and the arts of their respective countries, are signing a pact of brotherly friendship and look forward to ever more fruitful relations between their peoples.*'

'Gifts were exchanged. From a tall cabinet of florentine leather, almost without decoration and beautifully proportioned, a bronze lion appeared, a copy of the *Marzocco*, Florence's heraldic beast. Edinburgh replied with a volume of photographs of that city and a silver quaich, which the Lord Provost described as a Loving Cup, though he said he didn't know how the scots word could be translated: and indeed we all pitied any future italian guide trying to cope with so strange a noise when conducting visitors over the Signoría.

'Token gifts, certainly. But tokens of so much more than I, for one, or most of us indeed, had expected. Neither of these men was blethering. Both meant what they said. They won't let this gesture drop into a mere romantic gesture. They mean business. And that means, from both cities, a new and necessary dawn in the international sky.

'As a friend said to me afterwards: a Florentine, he said: 'I'ld love to spend a month in an Edinburgh home thinking of a scottish family doing the same in mine.

'We all talk these days about deepenings of international understanding, don't we? These men mean to do something about it.

'The Pact may well become historic.'

26 ❦

British Week

British Week in Florence in october 1966 was more than a trade show for british goods which had already been seen in other european cities.

There were two english pubs. One was called 'The Britannia.' It was put up like a pre-fab in the Piazza della Republica, more a country pub than a town one. Florentines bought thousands of glasses of beer, and only british residents winced at the price.[1]

The other was fitted up within a few days inside the independent basement of a café. This was decorated like a pub decorated like a castle. A scottish castle. But there was an english darts board. Florentines found this pastime funny but compulsive. They were not very good at it. But who is, the first time? Some young men, who may have been from Sicily or Sardinia,[2] flicked the darts from waist level like Paris apaches. Others started with a run like bowlers. Few regarded the foot line on the floor.

Thousands of shops displayed british goods, sold them and ordered more. A high proportion of these were scottish. Cloth, woollen goods, whisky. Especially whisky. Whisky bottles appeared in windows of shops that never sold drink:

---

[1] Three small glasses and two orangeades cost 17s.!

[2] On the other hand they may have been Florentines. An old florentine artist, contemporary with Picasso, has stories of street encounters in his youth which ended in knives.

pharmacies, lace-shops, even toy-shops. Whisky became as much a symbol of British as the Union Jack (which was never, that I saw, flown upside down). Florentines learned to discriminate between a malt whisky and a good private blend, between a good private blend and a commercial blend; and even among these last learned to view with scottish eyes brands named after royal oppressors of the Scots and one, named after a London street, which has been plentifully sold here in bars for years.

British biscuits (and even here Scotland was felt, since the majority of british biscuit manufacturers, wherever their factories may be, bear scottish surnames) were on sale in all kinds of unexpected places, even a milkman's shop on the outskirts, for months after. The taste of butter in them was a revelation to the Florentines.

Edinburgh sent a kilted pipe band and kilted highland dancers. Florentines were fascinated. The band and the dancers performed all over the place: on a tour round the city, at an immense party in the grounds of a museum, in an army barracks. There was a scottish, red, double-decker bus which left the central piazza for free rides, with a conductor handing out tickets. The british public, thought the Florentines, must be as orderly in fact as its reputation: for to prevent disorder florentine buses have one door for ingress and another, or two others, for egress, like Moscow's buses.

The Pearly King and Queen of London had real public presence and agreeable personalities in private. That both titles and costumes were hereditary through the female line impressed the Florentines, who got the impression that this had been going on since the days of the Florentine Arts. A London bobby took his turn at unflorid point duty: and two young policewomen further enhanced the british reputation for being civilised. They were attractive, and quiet, and authoritative without showing it. They met with respect, and a gleam in the male eye.

There was also a football match. This reassured the Florentines that the British were after all normal.

There was an unexpected effect. For a whole week Florentines strolled about the Centre, day after day, neglecting their work. They lingered and gazed and smiled at british sights. They were intrigued, entertained. They loosened up. They even got used to mini-skirts.

It was as if they had all gone abroad for a holiday. Old married couples went arm-in-arm as at the Cascíne. Young ones explored a new world. This was a seven-day festival for Florence. Britain seemed to belong here.

So british this atmosphere, that nobody would have been surprised to see, parting the crowds, british ladies in horse-carriages and crinolines, bowing from under parasols to english-speaking friends: or courteous explosive Walter Savage Landor taking his popular little dog Giallo into the café that dates from his time: or gentle, sallow, tiny 'Dear Isa' Blagden stepping the Via Tornabuoni on an errand to help a friend.

The victorian English may have been considered mad by the Florentines, but they were loved. Few who stayed were rich. In those days even a modest competence could cover at least one servant's wages and the hire of a carriage when required. Most of the colony were quiet and cultured and devoted to Florence and to the nascent Italy. What, one wonders, would they have thought of how far their hopes have been realised?

The british colony has dwindled today. It is no longer called mad, though it contains some eccentrics. The majority of its members are middle-aged or elderly, or have jobs here, or paternal investments, or have married Italians. The american colony has taken its place.

Some of the Americans are considered mad, because their riches are outwith the Florentines' ken. Most Americans here are rich. But despite their likeableness, their enthusiasms, and their generosity, it must be admitted that the american colony has not been loved as the english was. Its behaviour during the Flood altered this.

At the end of British Week we are only twenty days away from that dire disaster. We must prepare for it in a way the Florentines could not.

27 Rome

I have not been writing this book to prove anything nor to take sides about anything. But in the writing, chapter after chapter, up from amid the facts and feelings has come rearing a four-letter word: Rome.

Not Rome as a city, which three lifetimes and a library of books could not cover for acquaintance and understanding: but the government, of any party, which resides there. Not the people of Rome, who are warm and alert and forthcoming, uncles, aunts, cousins, friends: but the confused anonymity which administers Italy with paper issued from Rome.

Most italian cities, and much of today's italian culture, suffer from it. Authorities talk much about democracy and culture: but they have small respect for the individual, and what they mean by culture is a museum, and a state museum at that, like the Uffizi or the Etruscan Museum in Florence, under long-distance, faulty control.

Let us begin with small matters.

No government office will accept a personal cheque for any payment, although passing a dud cheque is a criminal offence in Italy. To pay a tax or for a radio or car licence, every citizen must spend time cashing a cheque at the bank and then maybe an hour in an overworked post office to fill out in quadruplicate a credit slip for the department's current account.

The loss of man-hours must be in millions.

If a public office has to communicate with a citizen, it never writes a letter, not even a registered one with evidence of delivery, as is common in legal and commercial circles. It sends a man, on foot to even remote houses, who presents a kind of summons, to be signed in person or by a deputy of the servee, who must then present himself at the office, open only in the mornings. Here he stands among other exasperated victims of democracy for half an hour or more, staring at shabby corridor walls and unable to sit down.

The cost of national man-hours must also be in millions: but The Law regards this not at all. The Law is no respecter of persons, not having been made for persons.

If a citizen writes to a public office to complain of a lost telegram, to have a new house numbered, to ask about customs duty, the reply is another summons to present himself. For italian bureaucrats not only respect nobody, they trust nobody. In their professional nightmares that a man who writes a letter may not exist, and so cannot be filed, they insist on seeing him, and often also his identity card which all must carry. When the body appears, they are often out to coffee.

No citizen can build a house (for which he will already have had permission) without a certificate of habitability. But it is no use just to apply for this. He must go to the Technical Office in person and pay L.3,000; then to the Health Office in person and pay L.3,000; and must then wait in a post office to pay L.10,000 into some current account in Rome. This, however, gives him no guarantee that the house is in fact habitable.

The reason for such public bumbledom is simple. It is dangerous for administrators to write a letter, which is written evidence, or to use the telephone, which is no evidence at all. But personal interviews can be to his positive advantage.

Each official act has to be drawn out as long as possible. We are still talking of small matters, such as for example the registration of a parcel.

The very receipt-forms and number-labels have neither gum nor perforation. A post office assistant has to cut out the vouchers with a pair of government scissors, then glue it on the parcel using a brush and a jar. The receipt also must be cut out by hand: but some more expert or more friendly assistants do, it is true, use the edge of a ruler, more or less neatly. This saves a few seconds for each of the ten or twelve people patiently watching.

The sad calm of any florentine public office is like that of a congregation contemplating the lonely coffin before a funeral service begins.

On the other hand, so great is the grip of government gum in post offices that many assistants from pure habit, instead of moistening postage stamps on a sponge, dab another layer on the already gummed backs.

Then comes fun with rubber stamps. Rubber stamps are of course requisite for quick dates and other identifications. It is right that post offices should whet their efficiency with them. But not only post offices have rubber stamps. Commercial firms, secretaries, presidents, representatives, schools, charities, art galleries, museums, professional men, even priests, they must all have their rubber stamp. And this must be circular. A letter or document with no rubber stamp or with a square or oblong one is dubious to invalid, and its sender has no standing. Shops that make and sell round rubber stamps are numerous in Florence as in all italian cities.

For if government offices take this attitude, everyone else for convenience must follow. It is like not accepting cheques. It is like eating too much garlic.

The simplest form of action involving the smallest measure of governing is secured, like a government contract, by personal introduction. In Italy almost everything official can be or must be so done. An anxious parent can ensure a higher examination mark for a nervous child by going to see the headmaster beforehand. Very few ordinary jobs or appointments can be obtained without somebody's word in somebody's ear: and almost no state ones. This is known as 'a recommendation.' Much talent in consequence goes unused into unemployment and poverty.

A foreigner arrives with a permit of sojourn for six months, having been firmly warned by a consul in his native land that in no circumstances can this possibly be extended. He finds, however, that it can be, if he presents himself at the *Questura* (police headquarters). Here he is given an extension for a month, reasonable for emergencies.

He now finds that by going to another person, not connected with the police but influential with them, he can get an extension for three months. At the end of that time, if he takes a day trip over a frontier, he will qualify for another three months. This he does regularly. At one time a train from Milan to Lugano was filled with foreigners doing so.

As he sits in his outward-bound train at the frontier waiting after having passed the passport control, he may notice an inward-bound train arriving at the next platform. He could easily nip across with pyjamas and toothbrush and save himself the cost of a night abroad. But if he has any sense, he will stay where he is. He might be recognised, refused re-admittance as a false tourist, held on suspicion of smuggling watches out of Switzerland or etruscan finds into Germany— he might even have to return to his native land for another six months' permit which would not be forthcoming.

Such trips, though not disagreeable, are expensive. And his permit now has two foolscap pages patterned with round rubber stamps like the haloes of the saints in a Last Judgment. Also the paper is disintegrating. He applies for a permanent permit.

This, reasonably enough, being on national level, must go to Rome. In preparation he is grilled. A police officer tries to trap him into betraying his real motive in wishing to stay in Italy. Plainly he suspects drug-passing or the white slave traffic. In the end, puzzled, he grants a permit for one month, which he hammers out himself on a typewriter with two fingers at a speed which would win a competition: but reluctantly, and with strict instructions for the foreigner to present himself without fail on the day of expiry. Rome is about to enter.

The foreigner is back where he started.

Prompt to the day he returns. Nothing has come from Rome. He is given another month and another warning. At the end of this, nothing has come. Punctually, month by month, he returns, getting to know well the pictures on the waiting-room wall and the clerk who is learning german to better himself: till the time comes when he arrives one day late.

His explanations and apologies are cut short. 'Don't worry about the exact day, Mister. Don't worry about coming here any more. When the permit comes through, we'll advise you. It's only Rome.'

Such reaction to the delays and frustration of head offices is far from uncommon. I could give more important examples, but do not wish to embarrass or endanger either men who do regard their work as a public service, or myself. But among the men on the job the frustrations do exist, as they did in my time at the BBC, blocking communication between provider and needer, cutting efficiency to a minimum, and rotting the individual in the name of nothing.

It has a positive side, in that a humane official who takes his job seriously, if faced with applying an unworthy law to a worthy case, can interpret the former his own way. This means rousing his sympathy and could lead to corruption. I am not sure that official corruptibility in Italy is as general as people say.

Certainly every now and then big scandals break on a high level, and are punished, if not always either punished or detected. A system which employs a needlessly large number of civil servants at necessarily small salaries to administer a paper law with little meaning for the cases handled is bound to make for some corruption: a further failure of the law to be made for the public, since corruption corrupts the corrupter.

And fiddling is widespread. A large number of taxation assessments are arrived at by official and taxpayer bargaining like Arabs, each friendlily aware of what the other is doing. Here, however, there is no corruption. Facts and figures can be fiddled, but not the law itself in most cases. The enormous mass of written matter required by the law leads inevitably to long delays, months and even years: and it is here that the bank notes pass, to bring a particular paper to the top of the pile.

A much worse aspect is the discrimination shown by officials between ordinary members of the public and favoured people. No political party has shown any sign of concern in Italy's official peril except the Liberals.

The Liberal Party has recently come out with a suggestion for a 'civic magistracy' to hear complaints from members of the public about their treatment by officials. But the courts it proposes could in practice do very little against the mammoth civil service protected by the Law, and might well be compelled to end by sifting complaints to a tiny minimum already actionable. The law in its present condition has forestalled most objections against itself: and before such courts acquired enough power it would be necessary to reform the very sections of the codes they are designed to modify. It would mean taking the mainspring out of the present law by statute: an excellent thing: but it would amount to drawing up an entire new code. This only a very strong political party could manage: and the Liberal Party, slung in its hammock between state monopoly and industrial and commercial combines, as in all countries today, has a small following even in Florence, the city of the small unit.

We are now among the larger issues, in the making of the law itself: and it may seem presumptuous of a foreigner to throw stones. Especially from his own glass-house.

The very first day that I studied the english law, an eminent professor gave us its two main principles. 'The law does not protect persons' he said, 'but property. Secondly, Never expound to a judge the justice of your case: he will want to know What is the law?'

That was forty years ago. Now the law does protect persons, or much more than it did. Which shows that case-law, modified by statutes passed by either of the prevailing political parties (and occasionally by a Private Member's Bill) does develop, slowly but organically, in the interests of the public. It would be stupid to attack Italy because she prefers another system; and I am not doing so. It is the running of that system which preoccupies the present chapter, because of what is to follow in later ones: concerning the people of Florence.

It must be confessed that most people in Florence worry themselves little about officials or about Rome. They are used to both. This has no connection with fascist trainings in fascist years. They have been used to meaningless outside controls since the French, the Dukes of Lorraine, the Vienna Empire. The present system they accept as part of the way things are: unalterable. They shrug, and say 'You know what we Italians are.'

Indeed the way things are does often seem unalterable: the Rule of Law dominating all parties, who alone can destroy it. The central chaos spreading down into the florentine *giunta*.

Business is held up, decisions are postponed, public needs neglected, for the sake of personal attacks by member on member from motives of political partisanship. The city *giunta* is little more than an executive body putting into action the will of the central government. There is also a provincial administrative *giunta* which rules all Tuscany in the same way. Local politics are ruled by national politics in all countries, unfortunately: but Rome is far less responsive to the needs of Florence than London is to those of Sheffield. And italian politics are chaotic.

Each party has a badge (a cross on a shield, an ivy leaf, the hammer-and-sickle and so on): useful shapes to guide inexpert electors, some of whom are illiterate, puzzled by the muddle of promises. At present the biggest party is the Christian Democrats, roughly equivalent to our Tories and full of mutual recriminations. About a third of the nation votes Communist, especially those who live by agriculture—which must make Stalin in Eternity leap for incredulous joy! There are many tuscan communist majorities and mayors. Fiesole has one: Florence had one. But the hammer-and-sickle appears in two other party emblems: that of the United Socialist Party, an uneasy fusion of two fractions, and that of the People's Socialist Party, which is marxist, leans to China and lies farther to the Left than the Communist Party. Besides Social Democrats there are Liberals, Republicans, Monarchists and the MSI (neo-fascists).

In a gaggle of splinter parties some kind of vexed coalition is inevitable, with the result that no party can ever put into force its full programme, or as much as is left after discounting election promises. The running of the country remains in the hands of the officials we have seen at work. Even the leader of a prevailing party is an unstable figure when any single coalition fails, and the President of the Republic spends sleepless nights looking for new premiers. The general public follows his moves with less interest than it waits for the day's lap-winner in the Giro d'Italia.

Of course things do ultimately get done. One day reservoirs will be built for Florence. A small aerodrome-airport is being put into use, which if it had been accepted years ago when first discussed, before the Autostrada del Sole was allowed to cleave the site in two, would now be of the size that Florence planned and needs. Someday the traffic problem will be solved, either by sealing off the Centre, or by large underground car-parks or lofty ones on many floors (if underground in the Piazza della Republica, interesting classical roman finds may be made). Meantime, true to mediaeval tradition, the *giunta* has brought in a foreign traffic expert in oneway streets.

Meantime also a coercive central state goes on coercing. It may indeed be true that Italians are less law-abiding than, for example, the British. But we did not spring suddenly so out of the soil as a gift from God to an expectant world. We grew so without a written constitution on the base of a monarchy limited by powerful barons in their own interests when monarchy was the best form of government. Our governing class then grouped roughly into government and opposition in a more or less two-party system. When more people were allowed to vote, this spread sideways, and our present State is the result of that. Italy has always had her state imposed on her.

Nobody is loyaller than I to the Risorgimento and the Unification of Italy, to bring about which Maresa's forebears gave famous help. But Italy has twice been let down by her own fine but mistaken patriots. The Liberals of the nineteenth century bowed her to Rome: no answer to the regional differences of the South, the Islands, of Florence. Mussolini imposed a stricter state. Democracy after his fall abolished fascists and the fascist outlook, but the state remained as it had been before him. No italian state has yet corresponded to the italian nation.

This chapter in no way advocates an italian copying of Britain, though it may be that if government is to continue, the italian parties may find it necessary to group into—say— three major parties, left, centre and right. But that is their affair, and no one national form of government can really apply to another nation. But sometimes I wonder if a United States of Italy might not be a solution: in which all regions would be autonomous, with the right to secede and the responsibilities of alliance. Then Florentines would be in-habitants of a modern city state, dependent on themselves, their fingers and brains, as in their great days but real in a modern world.

In a modern world it would not work. Industrialised Milan, for instance, might intrigue with shipbuilding Genoa to gain possession of Florence and her products: or Catania with Naples for a fruit monopoly: and Rome would probably plot with all of them to regain her position as capital. There might be a standardisation of bureaucracy worse than the present.[1]

In any case no other nation can be smug. We in Britain, with our services which, whether armed, civil, police, medical or other are indeed services to the public (I speak by comparison), cannot afford to be. The whole world, whatever the name for the way its parts are organised, fascist, communist, socialist, democracy american, democracy british or african, or any other, is heading for total bureaucracy. The next war may have to be fought for nothing more than a verbal definition of democracy: that will make little difference, whatever its outcome. For maybe two centuries mankind looks like being the slave of his own freedom.

At the end of that period it is conceivable that mankind may grow weary of both freedom and rulers, and the New Jerusalem descend out of Heaven merry with an absence of government. By which time, let us hope, Florence like the rest of mankind will be ready for anarchy.

Meanwhile Florentines, so far as the anonymity allows them, like Britons in the same measure, go on going their own way.

They had to do so, and did so wonderfully well, independently of Rome, after the flood of november 1966.

---

[1] A recent proposal by Rome to decentralise administration within certain limits may be a step in the right direction: but the same number, indeed the same persons of bureaucrats will merely be distributed topographically over the various localities.

28

A Sackful of Sand

An italian bicyclist was re-entering Italy. Besides a little suitcase strapped to his bracket he carried a small sack over his shoulder.

'What's in the sack?' asked the italian customs official.

'Sand.'

'Sand?'

'Sand.'

The official felt it. 'All right' he said, 'Pass.'

Seven days later the bicyclist appeared again with a sack on his shoulder.

'What's in the sack?'

'Sand.'

'What, you again?' The official opened the sack. It was full of sand. 'All right' he said, 'Pass.'

Again later the same bicyclist and the same official.

'Sand again?'

'Sand.'

'I don't believe you.' The official took the sack and went away.

After a while he returned, tying up the sack and marking it. 'All right' he said, 'It is sand. But what do you carry it for?'

'That's my business' said the bicyclist. Which was, so far as the customs went, true.

When this happened again, the whole customs house staff was alerted. They not only analysed the sand, they took the bicycle to bits and analysed that. Hours passed before the official came back. 'All right' he said. 'Pass' he said, glaring sourly and surly.

For many weeks nobody could find either diamonds or drugs or anything contraband. Then the official retired. He used to sit in a café and watch the tourist cars going by.

One day he spotted the bicyclist, still with a sack on his shoulder. 'Eh! *Signore*! Stop and have a little glass with me.'

He leaned across the table. 'Now, tell! Give!' he said. 'I'm not a customs official any longer. I won't denounce you. For interest, just what are you smuggling?'

'Bicycles' said the bicyclist.

29

The Coming of the Mud

I do not propose a picturesque description of the flood of 4 november 1966. The whole world, except perhaps communist China, was alert to it. Films and books were made about it. Help poured into it, with tergiversation only from Rome.

In twenty-four hours rain reached 200 millimetres, which is more than in all the days of october together, during which more rain had fallen than in six previous months. The average rainfall in a year in Italy is 800 millimetres.

That night of the third we had a guest, who arrived an hour late, sodden as if he had fallen into the sea, and had supper in my dressing-gown. His Alfa-Romeo had stalled in a small, darkness-hidden lake on the Via Bolognese. When I took him home, the water round the edge of this sudden pond reached half-way up my calves on the sloping highroad.

In the english fens I had been out on a minatory night, heaving sand-bags. There was no parallel whatever. Here the sky itself was evil. It was like the end of the world. A persistent cumulative malice of cloud.

Two hundred and fifty million cubic yards of water (some say, four hundred million) stampeded to the sea. They broke the Arno's banks. More stampeding herds jammed into the river from its tributaries, the Affrico, Mugnone, Mensola inside the city, the Sieve, Ombrone, Bisenzio and others above or below it. These too broke banks, avenging the sneers of summer visitors at their dry beds.

About a quarter of this mass charged into Florence at

40 m.p.h. through the places we have visited in former chapters. It closed-in east and west on Campo di Marte and Porta al Prato: it burst out south and north as far as the slopes of Bellosguardo, as far as the Via Larga. Two areas worst hit were Piazza Gavinana, a working class area on the left bank, where the river bends, and the people's square, Piazza Santa Croce, with all the small streets round it. It filled our small streets, their basements and *botteghe*, up to the first floors and even higher. The bronze doors of Florence's first heart, the Baptistery, rang like hammered bells. Some of the famous panels fell off them from the vibration.

Even earth joined in dissolution. Landslides all round, big or small, carrying a van into a gully, blocking lanes, burying one house and sloughing-off another down a field, where it stood entire for a day or two and then disintegrated.

What hit Florence was not just mad water, but mud, sand, refuse, trees, furniture, sewage, chemical substances, dyes, printers' ink, poisons and the heavy oil called *nafta* by Italians, who use it everywhere for heating houses. This nauseating abominable muck or slime got in everywhere, even into private safes in bank basements, which were fire-proof, burglar-proof, almost bomb-proof but not proof against this.

It was fiendish with force. Modern motorcars, being water-tight tins, float. The flood used them as battering-rams, tumbled them over like driftwood, stacked them in heaps. Two thousand of them became scrap in a morning. The suburbs were littered with their survivors, past repair, like cripples saved from a burning hospital with no beds free in any other.

Flood turns furniture into berserkers: civil war between tables, bookshelves, the television set. Bedsteads and wardrobes explode. In claustrophobic terror timber joins humans. Occupied coffins in the mortuary assault one another.

On the roof of the prison terrified convicts collected after an official *sauve qui peut*. Many, more in terror than in a dash for freedom, jumped into the current below and got away. One drowned. A group of others, mostly burglars, broke into a neighbouring convent and spent some hours there. They were given polite christian food, and later went quietly away. Some convicts managed to leave the country: but most could not take the flood, the cold, the isolation, their own fears; and either gave themselves up or were rounded up, not unwillingly, weeks later. Some, who made no attempt to escape, saved the lives of the Governor and his family and had their sentences reduced.

Lives were saved all over the city. Thousands, probably, by a decision of the *Prefetto*, a kind of civil governor, appointed by Rome to maintain law and order. In the early hours of the morning, having notice of the city's peril, he had to decide whether to sound an alarm or let sleeping men lie. He calculated that since it would be the dawn of a public holiday, few would be going to work in the streets. An alarm might start a panic, chaos, street-blocks of escaping households, a massacre. After this decision, which cannot have been easy, he was *incomunicado* in his Prefettura, as the Mayor was in the Palazzo Vecchio, without telephone or even the possibility of messengers. Had Florence been a disorderly city, this too might have worsened the disaster.

Many hundreds of lives were saved also by the city engineers, who a year or two previously had found the Ponte Vecchio ricketty and reinforced it. So for the second time this 600-year-old bridge stood up to omnipotent flood. And this was well: for the Arno narrows at this point, and had the Ponte Vecchio fallen, the dam so made might have diverted the flood-race and brought down the Uffizi itself with hundreds of houses both round it and on the other bank.

At one time, I was told, there was not a bridge to be seen above the surface of the Arno except the middle of one, well awash, and the superstructure of the Ponte Vecchio, like a howdah. Sturdy, wise old beast of burden! for days it bore, plastered above its arches where brackets held up the skeletons of the goldsmiths' shops, an entire tree.

Thousands more lives were saved by the mediaeval common stairs we have noticed. People withdrew to upper friends. And so the loss of life was relatively small: under fifty, it was reported. Of the exact total figure there is some doubt, because here accidental deaths are counted statistically only by bodies found already dead. More there certainly were, but how many more?

Nevertheless, Florence's still mediaeval system of living went heavily against the craftsmen and artisans, joiners, smiths, mechanics, in the small streets. They lost everything: not only homes and workshops but also plant and tools, jigs, welding irons, their possibility of working.

The result was a sudden silence.

In silence the loquacious Florentines swept and pushed. There were not enough brooms. In silence they used anything they had, fashioning pushers out of their own splintered doors and windowframes to get rid of the stinking slime. They were stunned. In silence an old cobbler devotedly took to pieces a small electric motor he had just afforded to simplify work. Two elderly women sat silent on a stone ledge. With nothing to sweep or push, they seemed waiting for something else.

In silence, when the first bridge was reopened, a group of young men surveyed the Arno over the parapet. 'You have been very naughty' they said. And poured in a sackful of coal.

The water did not stay long. The slime remained. The cold of it gripped legs in boots above ankle-height, knee-high in places. The stench of it was foul. People went with handkerchiefs to their noses or improvised surgeons'-masks of white gauze. Especially near the covered fish and meat market with its burst refrigerators below. Disease was imminent.

Disease was avoided by transportless doctors, visiting patients in gum-boots; and by the civic warnings; and by the self-discipline of the people in response to them. A single plate cleaned in filthy water, one mistake over excretion with no water, might have led to a deadly epidemic with medical services crippled. But there was not a single case of typhoid or typhus among half a million people. A doctor flew from London with big supplies of serum; more came from Holland. For many days voluntary helpers worked with syringes on whoever came.

Already on the afternoon of the first day food was distributed by the *Comune* in streets and piazzas: for there was a danger of famine. The Mayor had followed his predecessor's warning to shopkeepers about the Alpini: but there was small need of the warning. Grocers and other provision-mongers sold quietly at the usual prices to the queues which formed when it got known if there was still food to buy. The free food, when these shut up shop, could not be *pasta* or rice, the staple florentine dish: for there was no means of boiling it. Nor bread, either, because so many ovens had blown up. It was whatever else there was, or which could be rushed in by lorry from Bologna over the mountains where the roads were open.

Water too, to drink. In the first few hours private citizens with wells on the outskirts motored in with supplies of this in containers. Bottles of it were handed round by those who had it. The British Consul, among many others, was observed carrying several at a time. They were empty whisky bottles. Blissful reminders of British Week, so short a time before.

Among the first shopkeepers to disentangle and right themselves, to wash and disinfect their tiled walls, were the butchers, who got meat from Bologna: and greengrocers also, the fresh sweet healthy scent spreading out into the surrounding stench. In the short winter day, there being no electricity or gas, these sold by candlelight.

In this emergency the *giunta* turned human. Political parties were forgotten. Communists joined with capitalists. Priests and atheists together did much more than sit on joint committees. Class distinctions disappeared, because all classes had been hit. And in addition to the free food from the *Comune*, later, when cooking was again possible, many a contessa was to be seen preparing and serving free meals in a sort of super-soup-kitchen on waste ground, the materials supplied by themselves and their friends, possibly from country estates.

In all countries after elemental disasters of this kind the authorities turn to the Army, the Air Force, the fire brigade. With regard to the fire brigade, if in an earlier chapter I came to jeer, in this one I remain to praise. Without any reservations. For weeks and weeks it toiled day and night in repulsive and often dangerous conditions: and, so far as I know, without any special public recognition: like the undertakers during the London blitz.

Each day, for days, the gentle voices of helicopters sang in the sky of Florence. Strangely peaceful, like birdsong after a thunderstorm. They carried food to survivors on country rooftops or took them off ten at a time to big houses on the outskirts of the city. For if matters were bad in Florence, they were far worse out in the ocean which surrounded it, where the waters did not subside for many days, and no putrefying dead animals could be reached for destruction in the public safety.

The Army's is a less simple story. The very first day a regiment arrived from La Spezia to keep order. Martial law, almost; but not quite and not needed. There was a little looting, but not much: and the police stopped that. There was a little profiteering on the quiet: but the Army could not have discovered that, and the Mayor's warning had minimised it anyway.

Florence was lucky in this *Sindaco*. Piero Bargellini, the art-historian we have heard on the subject of Poll-the-Ox. He had not been long in office, and few thought he would be. Still fewer expected him to reveal qualities of leadership, indefatigability, realism, resourcefulness, as he did. He grew with the public need of him, as some men do: Winston Churchill, for example, in which respect these two had much in common. By a curious irony one of the first matters he had declared himself for in his first weeks was a campaign, well planned and novel, for cleaner florentine streets.

The Army, however, misunderstood what was wanted. It put soldiers on traffic duty, heavily armed. It sent amphibians. These swam the streets, struck submerged cars, and bounced off into first-floor windows as yet intact. It sent a column of lorries of soldiers armed, I was told by an eye-witness, with 'trowels.' These may have been trenching tools.[1] It patrolled the empty streets that night, looking for trouble that didn't happen.

In any case, when a general arrived from La Spezia next day, Bargellini re-assumed civil control. Florence, back to its great days, governed itself.

As a result of this visit the Army stayed a month and earned the gratitude of the city for its ungrudging non-military labours. Seventeen hundred men on the 10th of november swelled into 3,500 before they left on the 6th of december. They had cellars and shops in 700 streets to clear of mud. They had 300 tons of putrefied matter to burn with flame-throwers and 400 of decayed food in the market: not to mention corpses of race horses, dead inmates of the Little Zoo and other tragic animal relics in the Cascíne, and pets of all kinds in all kinds of holes and corners. In the market, despite gas masks, some soldiers collapsed. But in the streets they were the only merry people. They joked and laughed as they worked, and so raised the spirits of everybody.

The rumble of lorries bringing in food, blankets, medicines, from other cities was now magnified by arriving army pumps,

---

[1] Spoken Italian is contracting even faster than English. The words *pin, nail, cube box*, in their italian equivalents cover up to half a dozen meanings each, for which other languages retain more precise determinants.

bulldozers, grabs, cranes, excavators, drain-clearers and every kind and shape of apparatus, lorry and tanker. These did fine work. There were not enough of them.

Students arrived to help with the drying and cleaning of art treasures in museums, and of books and manuscripts in libraries, especially the National Library of Italy which has always been in Florence, and in the Accademia, where these had been vomited on by an exploding sewer.[1] They numbered over 5,000, from many universities in Italy and abroad, including Israel. Some spent a fortnight, some stayed till summoned home. They had no names and no money: but there was something of the young nobles of Monte Senario about them, only their work was done in mud-floored, stifling chambers, and their retreat was the railway station. They slept at night in six second-class unheatable coaches, four to a compartment, in a siding, which the stationmaster laid at their disposal. They fed in an equivalent of soup kitchens.

With them came bands of *capelloni*, as the Italians call the longhaired and often bearded successors to the Ted. Now the Florentines stopped staring at these hairy creatures, who laboured all day every day. They laboured into the night too, with candles. They refused to be paid, and refused to work for anyone who could pay. With their own hands they cleaned a large part of the small-street cellars before the Army with its machinery had finished those in the big ones. Their existentialism came to fruition here. This was their finest happening. And the poorer, thankful, wondering Florentines called them 'the angels of the mud.'

The early days after the flood recalled the London blitz during the second world war. There was a similar quiet determination, similar mutual help, similar neighbourliness, similar humour. 'Closed for the Holidays' read a notice on one

---

[1] In this book I am not concerned with the astounding way in which the world took the art treasures of Florence to its heart, and the generosity with which it saved so many of those threatened: but only with the people of Florence.

194

wrecked shop on the second day, like 'He's Broke Our Windows but Not Our Hearts' from the more sentimental Cockney. Similar anecdotes, too. 'A good thing we've got the Arno' muttered an old woman tipping mud and bits of her home bucket by bucket into it. And the flood-bore for the bomb-bore.

And the public services worked like those of London, heroically, at top speed. Under army searchlights which beamed all night from the Piazzale Michelangelo, sterner lights than those on St John the Baptist's Day (the pagan Festival of Water), water was restored, at first not for drinking, then chlorinated, then pure again; light and power for heating (even more important as the winter got colder); telephone communication; all these in an unexpectedly short time. A small part of the Santa Croce area even had some electricity by the 10th of november!

The Florentines, who naturally made no parallel with the London blitz, were reminded of the *Emergenza*, the German Occupation. During that, there was the same instinctive help given. A certain lady, who sheltered Bernard Berenson, and by a trick many of his best pictures, in her house,[1] found herself and all her children too now at work every day cleaning books in the National Library.

For recovery came amid forebodings and uncertainty.

Many of our small streets had façades shored up by immense baulks, either grouted into the roadway at an angle or bridging across horizontally to other unsafe houses opposite, skeleton Bridges of Sighs. In one of these, the Via de' Neri, the inhabitants covered over the timbers with green foliage as Christmas drew near, and set a Christmas tree on top with coloured lights. A serene defiance: for their cellars were still unusable and insanitary. A vain defiance. Some weeks later the timbers fell, crushing a van that was passing.

Florentines were anxious. The weather continued dirty;

---

[1] As may be read in a recent book called *The Consul of Florence*.

rain and fog, fog and rain. On the 10th of november people sat up all night expecting another high water with the broken banks as yet untouched. Within some weeks the Ombrone again overflowed. Nobody was convinced that the danger was ended.

Nor could anyone do anything but wait. The Arno does not belong to Florence but to an organ of the central Ministry of Works called officially and without irony the 'Civil Genius.' Its local branch has large premises that sprawl over part of Lorenzo de' Medici's garden. Year after year fields are flooded downstream from Florence, and the city has been flooded many times, more than once seriously, and once almost as drastically as in 1966. The Civil Genius had done nothing ever to prevent flood. It had no waterchecks, systems of level measurement or other controls. It had no representative at the two dams about thirty-five miles upstream which were built for a hydroelectric scheme. The hydroelectric engineers had no communication with the Civil Genius in Florence; and no powers to hold back water, only to make electricity. On the night of the spate, seeing their level phenomenally high, they did their duty to protect the dynamos from a dam-burst and opened the gates. Hence a large part of the reason for the weight of the blow which hit Florence suddenly.

The Civil Genius rebuilt the banks, a little stronger than they were in the time of the Grand Dukes. But if they have plans for treating these provincial floods at the great expense needed, little or no publicity has been given to them. Nor has any to its regrets, if it ever expressed any.

The task of clearing the mud became more and more difficult. In some streets what had been removed in the day-time rose up and flooded back in the night. Under them lay a drainage system of Dante's time, and nobody knew where it passed or went. The whole drainage-system of the city, never big enough (an explosion on the left bank in the previous

196

summer was not yet repaired) had to be opened and relaid. The going of the Army left Florence with these problems, not enough manpower to solve them with, not nearly enough machinery, and no material help from Rome. By the middle of march, left to her own resources, she divided herself into thirty districts and got on slowly with the final freeing of herself from mud.

Slowly as the mud itself. By this time Bargellini[1] was fighting not only bureaucracy but the *giunta* too. The old central parties started up again their old irreconcilable prejudices. Recriminations, insults, personal accusations wasted again the time for deliberation, and crippled action. One communist member even laid official information against the Prefetto for not warning the city.

The plight of fat folk and thin folk alike worsened.

Tobacconists, for instance. Rome not only did not help their recovery, it actively hindered it. Tobacconists, who sell also salt, postage stamps, and other government monopolies, were forbidden by some antique law distrusting even state employees, to throw out ruined stock before some government inspector had troubled to check that it had been ruined. No such government inspectors came. Perhaps they had not had official notice from Rome that there had been a flood in Florence, so could not come. But tobacconists could not live without selling, nor sell till their shops and cellars were cleared and cleaned and disinfected and certified as such. The state monopoly, on the other hand, had no power by its own law to alter its own law. In the anonymity of Rome nobody had. After weeks of exasperation and growing want a local MP had to travel to Rome and force the state to take note of the flood.

---

[1] Bargellini is one of the few members of his political party who is almost a complete Christian (he would agree with the adverb) and a convinced Democrat.

Within a year a splinter party by abstaining from a vote of confidence on petty political grounds pushed him out of office. There is here no historical parallel with Churchill.

State offices continued not only to neglect but to embitter ordinary citizens by small, unnecessary exactions. Radio licences for 1967 had to be paid for in advance on sets that had no future, having been destroyed in november; unless notice had been given by a certain time with proof of destruction. Who thinks of radio licences when they are exiled to a cousin's overcrowded flat or wearing cast-off clothes in an Institution with no means of earning the next thousand lire? But that was The Law: and nobody was un-complacent enough to modify it.

Other state crimes of omission were graver. According to The Law no member of the legal or medical professions was entitled to any relief whatever. In Italy the medical profession includes general practitioners, surgeons, consultants, psychologists, dentists, radiologists and others essential to the health of a city. In general they do not live on ground floors in the centre. Nevertheless fifteen of them had their homes, consulting rooms, books, cars and instruments totally destroyed and had to work with less equipment than a horse leech till they could borrow a stethoscope. Thirty others lost much: forty-five were affected less seriously. What was worse, X-Ray plant, cancer plant and other costly necessaries were destroyed. There was no state relief for these either.

The *Ordine dei Medici*, roughly equivalent to our British Medical Association, did raise a fund for loans from practitioners in other places. But this was soon finished. The members of a medical women's club in South Wales, finding they had an annual surplus, sent a cheque for a florentine medical family's use. This was accepted with the same grace as prompted the giving. But many medical men were too proud to ask for help, and the exact figures will never be known.

The spirit of the professional classes may be further seen in the journalists. The local newspaper, *La Nazione*, celebrated its centenary a year or two ago, having been in existence since the Unification of Italy, which it did much to create. Only a week or so before the flood it had moved from its cramped works and offices in the centre to spacious, airy, ultramodern premises on one of the avenues. This was near the river. Its *dernier cri* presses and machinery were wrecked: its offices unusable.

The staff had managed to get out an issue with news that the Arno had broken its banks: but little of that was ever distributed. Next day they were in Bologna getting out the first flood issue with the help of a Bologna paper. Before long mechanics were seen patiently dismantling the new plant in Florence and cleaning it piece by piece. Within a few weeks the editor had succeeded in raising the equivalent of several score thousand pounds for flood relief, which was distributed in gifts of about £57 a head to all who applied.

Rome too promised sums for every family flooded out, to replace furniture, tools and gear. When this credit arrived (or part of it) application to qualify had been reduced to an impossibility, if not an imposture. Rome feared being cheated. The applicant must either go to a notary-public (and he with little cash in his pocket for fees, indeed little for his family, or he need not apply) together with four independent witnesses not connected with his family, who would make affidavits that they had actually seen each article on the list of things lost: or he must produce photographs of the furniture, tools and gear *in situ* showing they had been his.

Out of the 500 million lire estimated to give each flooded-out family something far below the sum it needed, less than a tenth part had arrived by may of the following year; and there was much scepticism if any more would follow.

In the meantime the need of the smaller men in the small streets was immediate, and as the flood receded in time, became more urgent. At the beginning there had been free issues of food, blankets, bedding, clothing, and other bare necessities. These were welcome: for many and many had only the overalls they wore, and a winter to face. They came from other cities in Italy, from luckier people in Florence, from all over the world. But in the end they stopped. The future, both near and distant, took their place: a blank and heavy future.

Something near 23,000 families suffered physically and mentally. Out of 10,000 shops, 6,000 had been destroyed. Small shopkeepers and craftsmen could not get credit, because suppliers and middlemen had been ruined too. Of course, there were instances of manufacturers in other cities advancing goods to trusted old clients, but it was not general and did not happen at once. A moratorium was declared on payment of rents and other dues: but debt is a monster which grows the bigger the more it is repelled. The city fathers of Florence had not the means to help: and Rome was helpless. It was plain that, as ever, Florentines must go their own way, now a weary one, by themselves.

This was not so easy as in earlier centuries. On the one hand, the needs of the smaller folk were as primitive in those days as in the middle ages. Many were living on their cousins and relatives in overcrowded conditions: some were living where they could, separated from their families. Their homes were either uninhabitable from mud or so damp that habitation would be dangerous. But almost all of them had one yearning: to get back to them. Some squatted in a large unfinished building estate on the left bank, inside walls without heating or windows. For these, though they had built the premises for other purposes, some contractors finely laid on as many comforts as they could. The problem of re-housing, even temporarily, was so complicated by the return to party politics and vested interests that practically nothing was done.

In all classes everyone affected by the flood looked to a long-term future of life-savings diminished or quite gone, and months and years to pay off instalments on goods already destroyed, and longer years for new ones when they could get them. But the smaller folk, the artisans, once their savings were finished, if they had had any, could not feed their families if they did not earn: they would not earn if they could not work: and their means of work wcrc at the bottom of the Arno on the way to Pisa.

Florentines are not beggars. They shrink from charity. They carried themselves with self-respect even to an extreme. One very wide-shouldered flood-refugee, presenting himself where clothes were being distributed, could find nothing to fit him except a dinner-suit someone had sent. This he refused. 'How can I go about clothed like that? I would be laughed at.' In this he had neither gratitude nor ingratitude: nor did the volunteer reproach him. She cast about among her friends and was able to equip him decently. By florentine standards he was right.

There was a fund administered by the Chamber of Commerce. But this was only for such as were registered as artisans: and very many, either to escape taxation or for other reasons, never had registered. For them there was no official relief.

Of the rest, when they had bought their tools, many started back to work in cousins' livingrooms. Others walked back to their *botteghe* and plied their trade on wobbling relics of benches and broken chairs by candle light with the mud still round their feet.

They were going their own way home.

30

City to City

The Pact of Twinship, from which we expected action not sentiment, proved itself at once. Of course, Edinburgh was not alone. Hundreds of cities, small towns, villages, institutions and individuals all over the world sent whatever they could, whatever their intuitions or experience told them would be needed after a Flood. From the very first morning, when, I am told, a BBC announcer woke the eastern hemisphere with the news that the world at that moment was losing one of its greatest treasures, the world showed practically that Florence was not just a place to visit on holiday but one of the world's hearts, whether visited or not.

If I compiled and described all the help sent, this chapter would be a very large volume. So I deal little with the art treasures and much with the people of Florence. But if I compiled and described all the help sent to them, this chapter would far outweigh those already written and burst the covers of this book. So I choose, I hope not too arbitrarily, one or two symptomatic trends. And of these the first must be Edinburgh's help: for her twin sister was in trouble, and she acted with unforgettable promptitude.

Unless I am mistaken, the first load of help by air was blotting paper and talcum. This was for the slimy bricks in library basements which had to be turned back to books. And this immediately, before they dried themselves into gault blocks for ever. There were thousands of them; many were rare and illustrated; and each page had to be delicately separated, powdered and interleaved. The small exact fingers of a child of eight were as useful as the thick nervous fingers of an aged expert. The helpers stood ankle-deep in sawdust and in rooms so hot they might have been bombarded by a dozen hairdriers. Edinburgh's promptitude, like other promptitudes, literally saved these treasures.

Before a week was out, and within two days of the asking, fifteen hydraulic pumps arrived. Five hundred blankets arrived in the wag of a sheep's tail. More blankets arrived, for although the Red Cross was distributing blankets, there were never enough. This was timely; so were the medicines of all kinds; so was the baby linen. For when you are talking in tens of thousands of homeless people in one spot, where wholesale and retail chemists have been wrecked, and there are no stocks more of linen goods or lengths of linen, one diabetic must find his insulin;[1] and in 20,000 inhabitants there are many more than one: while the number of nappies needed has to be imagined.

Within three weeks, six propane drying machines from Edinburgh began to blast at sodden walls. This gift also was timely: for after a place had been dried and disinfected, the damp which had soaked down into the ground continued to rise like sap in a tree: a threat to several irreplaceable frescoes and a hindrance to rehabitation. Before long, batteries of this artillery were roaring away everywhere.

Perhaps the timeliest and most thoughtful of consignments were the portable kerosene stoves. These arrived in batches of 300 till over 2,000 families had the comfort of them. The *Comune* was giving out stoves; but these were clumsy, needed stove-pipes and sometimes holes in walls, and did not all work well. The portable ones used little fuel, and needed no ventilation. They radiated warmth and dryness in a complete circle and could be placed anywhere. Their recipients felt no

---

[1] A specialist in diabetes, realising that in the food shortage some might be tempted to eat things containing sugar and starch, stood outside his consulting room distributing insulin. A diabetic old lady, bewildered by floods and largesses, asked him for a kilo of beef.

longer abandoned, but cared-for at a great distance, and so were encouraged to face a winter of weak sun in a moist sky.

Individual gifts cannot all be mentioned here. The most touching gift of all came from Aberfan, where children's toys and clothes were sent by parents who had tragically nobody any more to play with or wear them. But children's clothes came also from the twin city, where a lady of over eighty freed her wrists from arthritis enough to knit them herself. And help came from protestant Edinburgh to a protestant church.

The famous churches of Florence soon had plenty of help: the congregations set to work to clean and repair the humbler ones. But it takes more than willing hands to repair a broken altar or replace its furnishings: and money was scarce. The Waldensian Church[1] had recently bought a second-hand fane in a part of Florence not flooded: but the school which it ran for its congregation's children was badly damaged. A cheque from Edinburgh helped its winter heating.

The Pact of Twinship had indeed become historic.

City responded to city from all over the world, institution to institution, individual to individual. I would like now to turn to one group of people in Florence which became a channel for institutions and individuals: but always remembering, please, that this was only one of several groups in Florence and that it channelled only a part of the flood of money arriving to relieve the continued suffering of Florentines.

A day or two after the flood some six or seven british and american residents decided to raise a little money quickly by writing to their friends abroad. Their talk took place in the

---

[1] The Waldensian is perhaps the oldest of all protestant churches. If not from farther back, as some of its members claim, it certainly dates from the Càthari of the twelfth century, whom we met by the curious pillar in the chapter on small streets. One of its tenets is that Elders should have power to sit in judgement on Ministers: in which it is very close to the presbyterian Church of Scotland. It centres chiefly in some valleys in Piedmont, where a massacre took place in the seventeenth century: which excess of 'the Babylonian Woe' caused Milton to write a sonnet.

British Consulate, because as it happened the American had been flooded and the U.S. Consul-General, a quiet but observant man, had only just arrived in a strange city. They hoped to distribute a few thousand lire immediately to certain grave cases they knew of. They had no written constitution, no calculated procedure: it was an informal indeed amorphous gathering headed by the British Consul, Christopher Pirie-Gordon.

I imagine that anyone interested enough to read this book will already have heard of this personality. But he became so legendary a figure in the city of my adoption that I cannot help indicating the kind of man he is.

Tall, with a deep voice seldom raised above a whisper, except for sudden, violent laughter which first startles and then stimulates others to laugh with him, he at one time sported a monocle. The british press took note of this, and for a time the monocle was not seen again: not, in fact, till flood relief ended and there was no more danger from the press.

With the manners of an old-english gentleman and the allusive wit of an Oxford don, he was a kind of office-bound Scarlet Pimpernel. He seemed as vague and formless as the group that collected itself under him: but people who acted or suggested action on their own initiative often found to their surprise that they were doing or saying exactly what he had already anticipated and expected.

He was a religious man, but not expressly. He had charity in its real sense: there must be no prejudices of any kind, no discriminations, and truly no one must be turned away from any door. Whether he had anticipated one particular case, I do not know: but a florentine lady who had lost both home and means of work turned out to be a prostitute. His christian attitude had spread to the other members of the group; and the magdalen received her small sum like anyone else.

But the chief door in question was that of the Consulate: which put burdens on the Consulate staff when word got round that there was money being given out. Not even the *carabiniere* on duty at the entrance could stem, control or silence the vociferous crowds. It put burdens also on his General Committee of Principal Residents (the capitals are mine: this was as informal as anything else): for he allowed almost anyone who happened to be in Florence and was interested in flood relief to attend its meetings. These grew so large and confused that they were abolished and the working group continued as before. This too he may well have foreseen.

One thing that neither he nor anyone foresaw, however, was the swelling of the fund. Money swept in like winds from all four quarters at once. When it died down, it rose again. Week after week. Word got round that any sum sent not to the Red Cross nor the italian government nor even to the Mayor of Florence but to this anonymous group would be passed on to a worthy destination at once, and direct, and intact. Which word was true, as we'll see.

American contributions, to comply with american income tax law, were routed through the American Church, which passed them in a few hours to the group for distribution. These had to be distributed to individuals with full particulars kept of every recipient. The same particulars were kept of british contributions; but these could also go to institutions such as the little orphan schools we have already met in an earlier chapter, or an important section of the lunatic asylum, or a training school for the deaf-and-dumb. The group was able also to put some institutions in touch with their equivalents in Britain directly: such as the Boy Scouts Association or the National Institute for the Deaf. The first boy scout troop of deaf-mute boys in Italy was thus enabled to celebrate its twentieth year six months after the flood with some uniforms and equipment partly as they had been before the flood carried them all away. A school in Newport, Monmouthshire, took a financial interest in a florentine orphan school. And so on. But such institutions in Florence also helped the group to find cases of special hardship among the permanently disabled, the blind, the victims of poliomyelitis and lifelong invalids, and elderly people brought into nursing-homes by policemen or doctors straight out of the flood waters.

For it was individuals who counted most, and not only for american taxes. They soon ceased to become cases: they became clients, or responsibilities, or friends. The group had three principles, stated at the beginning and never altered. They assisted those in dire need, and as a result of flood damage, and their assistance came immediately in small sums without waiting on the possibility of bigger ones. The actual circumstances must be vouched for by some responsible person in the neighbourhood, but without any definition of what constituted a responsible person.

In effect this was often the parish priest; sometimes, in out-lying districts, the village policeman; most often a lay member of the Order of St Vincenzo de' Paoli, patron of hermits in the fifteenth century. These lay members, however, were far from hermits. I was once present at one of their meetings; and over half were lawyers, doctors or other prominent citizens of Florence. They devoted their spare time to the relief of suffering of all kinds irrespective of class or faith or absence of faith. Having done so most of their lives, they knew everyone in the area they worked in.

These, as a starting point, provided lists of urgent cases. But very soon the Consulate doors and the Consulate letter-box[1] were crammed with other applicants, who had to be screened in case of fraud. The work was too much for the group members and the members of the order: so amateur 'field workers' were obtained. The city had been divided into zones, allotted to each of the group members, and these became leaders (the Americans called them 'Captains') each of a squad which examined every case personally and made

---

[1] Figuratively, this. Florence does not have letterboxes.

recommendations for or against payment by what they found. Within a week of this work the group had become experts.

It was an all-time job for everybody: and some of the group having daytime jobs of their own, could be in attendance only at night. The Consulate was kept open long after its usual hour of closing. Field workers clustered. Case sheets multiplied. Large rooms were lent by the Consulate, and its patient, unsquabbling, selfrenouncing staff shut away in corridors and cupboards. Nobody grumbled.

By the end of two months the group had distributed £40,000 in sums of about £20 as immediate first-aid. The total cost to the fund was the almost incredibly low figure of 0·0042%.

Every payment was made through the banks by a voluntary band of accountants from Superbox Ltd, a subsidiary of Metal Box Company. They authorised payments at the rate of sixty-two each evening, after their own day's work. This lasted for sixty evenings. In a rush to get as many payments as possible to as many people as possible before Christmas, they even one night reached 155 payments before staggering home to bed. They were not trained accountants, just intelligent and careful men and girls.

During the six months that this group worked, there were no rifts, jealousies, lobbyings, whisperings: not even minor national jealousies between the equally numbered British and Americans. There was no need, because there were no departmental officials. Most of them received initial shocks at the hideousness of some lives they came across. As these continued to come in, several who had taken refuge in an armour of impassivity, found themselves more and more involved and responsible; with a consequent sapping and straining of nerves. But this is normal in such activity, and the group remained ordinary people on a joint adventure, friendly, competent, sharing an expanding expertness.

Their informality was so efficient that when yet larger sums were brought from the USA by a former US Consul-General Merritt Cootes, these also were processed through the group's apparatus of names, visits, counterchecks and indices. At one time it looked as if the new american funds would be choked by formalism in New York: but thanks to the vigorous protests of this ex-Consul-General that peril was avoided in the end and at the end. By then 3,678 families had been reached with a total of relief equal to over £62,000.

They handled, or were in touch with, other funds. Iris Origo raised, mostly in America, a large total for distribution expressly among the *artigiani*. This was split into much larger cheques than the Anglo-American Committee could manage: so when it had claims too big for its resources, it sent them round to FAF. By this time it had had to co-opt others. Claims by *artigiani*, which continued to come in, were scrutinised by a new resident who had had professional experience in the British Commonwealth.

Another category of losses was in sewing machines: and for this a married couple with professional experience was co-opted. They persuaded a celebrated european firm of manufacturers to give special concessions and terms to victims of the flood. And this linked up with Lord Hastings' Fund for the Italian People.

Lord Hastings in London, coming rather later into the field, when the immediate enthusiasm for Florence had a little abated, raised a considerable sum, which was divided between the Florence neighbourhood, the neighbourhood of the Po mouths in Veneto, where in addition to bursting rivers the sea itself had broken in, and the Maremma, where a bigger River Ombrone had all but eliminated the land settlements we have spoken of. He was more concerned with rural suffering: but here also the group was able to help. One member, an authoress and working at a job in Florence, had charge of the biggest zone: that of the periphery and environs of Florence downstream to the west. She had no car; and the only means of getting to her charge was by infrequent bus or begging the local priest to fetch her. In the process she discovered a village called San Mauro, one of many on the road to Pistoia, where the Arno had not only made the poorish soil of the small-holdings unfit for cultivation, but had destroyed the sewing-machines for making straw goods (to which we have already referred) by which the village economy was actually maintained. Lord Hastings adopted this village through the group, and supplied it with replacements of chickens, rabbits, ducks and a calf or two, besides a couple of hundred sewing-machines new or repaired.[1]

The group knew well that they had given temporary treatment to only a fraction of an injured body corporate. When the fund came to its end, most of them were depressed, for they knew personally of many, many families whose need was as great and immediate as those who had been helped. But they accepted the principle of luck, and thereby became in part themselves florentine. In the Maremma, which if not florentine is at least tuscan, when pigs were given out, lots were cast for each. This was regarded as fair by everyone. One is lucky, another not. And so it was with flood relief in the city.

The group respected the spirit and locality of Florence, and was thereby able to restore part of her potentiality for abundance. What was more important, its and the other funds confirmed the Florentines' belief in the value of their city. They welcomed help to what they were part of, even if the luck passed them personally by, just as they have always welcomed compliments to their city more than to themselves. And the greatest of all compliments, and reassurances, was now to come from Rome.

In Rome there is a dyarchy that governs Italy. Of this the state stayed where it was. The Church came to Florence.

Alone with his secretary the Pope arrived on Christmas Eve

---

[1] Including american funds, the equivalent of £180,000 was distributed.

in a pealing of bells. He stopped in Piazza Gavinana. Alert to people amid their facts, he shook hands, he gave his first blessing. Then, as his big Mercedes moved to cross the river, he observed everything, mud streaks on walls, broken shops, silent Florentines gently applauding, awaiting they did not know what.

In Piazza Santa Croce, the people were standing, with *Adeste, Fideles* floating out of the opened doors of the wrecked basilica. Overhead floated bunches of yellow and white balloons (the Vatican colours), reminders of the Cascíne and other festivals of the people. So huge these bunches of gas-filled grapes, that their vendors had taken care not to scrape upperwindows in the narrow streets by which they came. Dozens of balloons, held by young and old, floated up in the floodlights as His Holiness appeared, up into the dark sky where an almost full moon suddenly parted drifting mists. Nobody knelt. People made little remarks of affection and admiration. Sober Florentines.

No pomp or circumstance. Only a short line of Boy Scouts and students in boiler suits holding flaming tapers, and one small boy in a red jumper. It was homely.

The Pope was homely. He seemed like one of the crowd, as halfway up the steps he turned and opened his arms, bright in scarlet and white among the sober Personages at the church door, and with a full, generous smile. The applause that had crackled over the Piazza turned to a great tattoo.

The Pope did not orate. He spoke. Telling of his love for Florence, he reinforced the Florentines' pride in Florence. The shuttered shops echoed louder applause when he ended by saying he himself was now a Florentine, and signed his name in the City Chronicles.

To him were presented invalids from a hospital-workhouse for the aged nearby, and other dwellers in that shattered district. Then he came down and talked to unselected people in the crowd. Then, always standing in his opened car, he went to rest and to meet prominent people in the Archbishop's Palace opposite the Baptistery. A crowd waited there outside, watching the flashes of newspaper camera bulbs through an upper window. But it was a long cold wait.

Hymns and bible-readings over a public address system, however well done, were not what the crowd had come for. Most of it melted away. It was himself they had waited for; and to those who persevered, his ultimate appearance at the window was a red candle in a homeless night.

Christmas midnight mass in a Duomo so bright that the pale frescoes were visible up in the Cupola, had an atmosphere more intense, but for all the spectacular robes and exquisite singing, it was homely too. The Pope celebrated it with the Chalice presented to him by the President of the Republic two years before, which now bore an inscription that it had been used in Florence this Christmas Eve, 'as an everlasting pledge of *benevolenza*.' With an everlasting niche, too, for the personal lives of the congregation, in St Peter's.

He did not intone. He spoke simply, like a broadcaster, giving each word its own unique meaning. In his discourse, which began ecclesiastically, he spoke as a human being of Florence's human problems, assuring his proud hearers that it was no offence to that pride to accept stupendous help from the rest of the world. His sturdy voice took on authority as he warned against laziness and 'decadent acrimonies.' And this was psychologically right. The Pope knew Florence. In these early days he sensed her dull despair.

That night the spirit of Florence was encouraged to go the way the Florentines wanted to feel was right. They needed to be told. They needed the human in the authority. It was this they had been waiting for: and seldom had the Christmas message of God-made-human arrived so timely in an evangel so warm and realistic. May the state take heed!

Reassurance on reassurance of the value of their city: it was this which avoided a revolutionary situation, although many of the elements of a revolutionary situation were present: a locality faced with danger and hunger, to be avoided or relieved only by government action; a disinterested or incompetent government acting only with promises under laws passed for its own sake not the people's; no help from the government and no hope for themselves. . . . But absent now was the feeling that there was nothing to be done.

And they trusted Bargellini, because Bargellini trusted them. Even in later days, when streets were closed, excavated and left unusable for weeks, a deterrent to shoppers, a further prolongation of unearning time: when a recently relaid Lungarno was dug up again to put new drains down: when months after the water had gone, the foul dread odour of that unforgettable mud came out like Apollyon at passers-by and further postponed home-coming, they still trusted him.

There was an attempt at an instigation, at a mass meeting-to-be in the old fish-market. Instead of thousands, a handful of bystanders watched three men inside sandwich boards. The Communist Party repudiated this fiasco, and no doubt if there had been such support the turnout would have been bigger.

But in place of revolution Florence set about recovery.

The first defiant gesture had come from the Opera as early as the last days of november. On the open stage of the Teatro Comunale stood the whole cast and all the theatre staff: open, because the front curtains had gone and there were no more wings. The dress of the chorus had had only part of the mud brushed out, mud that seemed never to come out of cloth. The costumes of the principals came on loan from La Scala in Milan. The shoes of the audience were muddied too, as they stepped across the pavement into the derelict foyer. Before Monteverdi's first notes were heard, this audience was moved to tears. Maybe not all of it were victims of the flood: but the Earl of Cork and Orrery would have wept with them.

Commercially, Christmas came too soon. The bigger shops,

and those which were branches from other cities, re-stocked themselves: some even had electric light in their windows. But few people, even among those untouched, felt like celebrating with purchases, except in a quiet way. And the smaller, independent shops had had all their christmas stock already waiting in the cellars. What replaced that, when shelves could be put up, was a token stock; and little of that was sold. The brave new christmas lighting of shopping streets which the city had instituted with competitions and prizes, there was no electric current for.

Florence set herself Easter as the date when she must be ready for tourists. She kept this vow. Little by little recovery showed. Wheels, cleaned and oiled, began to go round. Panes of glass were fitted into new or repainted frames. A street that had had one *bottega* open now had one *bottega* closed. Only those gaps, where an owner was no longer fit enough to carry on, and the streaks of oil, sinister yellow-brown, 6 feet high in places, 12 feet high in some, showed a visitor any trace of what had passed by those walls or of the suffering still going on inside. And the experts said, of the oil streaks, that the stone was too porous; they would never be removed.[1]

Then spring returned, drenching the hills in the pale perfume of wistaria. A wet spring, as it had been a wet winter. Damp houses remained damp, and entire streets were left untouched, awaiting their turn. But there was possibility in the air for the luckier and the stronger. In the piazzas, along the avenues between mud-black leaves of evergreens fresh leaf buds, incredibly, broke. On the drying bed of the Arno willows grew sideways over smashed, half-buried things. From the poor man was taken, by the cruel economic law, 'even that which he hath.' But the poor man was used to that. It was home that counted, even with one borrowed bed and a candle stuck in a bottle.

[1] In fact, however, the streaks and stains have faded into the stone and little is left of them. The stones of Florence breathe again.

There was a young house-painter who lost house and all. He had three young children and his wife was expecting a fourth. In the first moment of panic he lost his head, and his nerve, and his reason too, and tried to commit suicide. When he got out of hospital, he thought better. The house was not yet habitable but he made it so, borrowing tools to remake chairs and table, rewiring the fridge, polishing the useless television set. His family and his mother washed and repaired curtains, painted the walls and ceilings, not a hand idle. In this scene of industry he was tactfully asked how he felt about the future. 'Eh!' he replied with a confident grin at the fact, 'I'll be all right now. I'm at home.'

Do we recall the hallucinated carpenter with eight children who thought his home was being taken from him?

Do we recall that in the middle ages they burned the homes of the families they had exiled or slaughtered?

Where the home is, there is the florentine life. The life of a people who has not changed greatly at the heart of a city which has changed little, in 600 years.

31

The New Generation

Let us not romanticise the florentine home. The move toward freedom is the same here as everywhere else. As yet there may be few young men with long[1] and well-kept locks, gay-coloured clothes, stove-pipe trousers, and a longing for peace and fair living in the world's protest against sterility, stuffiness and stupidity. As yet the girl in the mini-skirt is lonely here unless she is foreign.

But make no mistake. The new generation of Florence is alert to the failure of our world. Already it has taken action, to the horror of its elders.

Florence's recovery was going to time. Small hotels and *pensioni* had been cleared of refugees and were accepting bumper bookings for the post-flood summer. In particular, because of british restrictions on travel abroad, it was Americans who planned to come. (Germans, the third tourist power, as a rule make few bookings: they bring their own food, and camp.) Americans would all have been given a special welcome after the flood-time generosity of America's people. Those who did come, found it so.

But modern war reaches every place that is still at peace. When the Israel–Egypt conflict moved into action, Americans in Florence, who were about to buy villas or invest money otherwise, refrained. Students of Florence, however, remembered the students of Israel who had worked with them in the libraries. They returned that help in donations of blood. They

[1] In all classes italian male heads have always had a wider choice of longer hair than british or american without eccentricity or special self-expression.

detested Egypt's dictator's scrambling vaunts and scuffling violence. They deplored all war and our world full of wars.

Against the maintenance of it in Vietnam they protested in public. Outside the American Consulate they overturned american cars. Arrests were made. People feared a riot. Some wrote exaggeratedly of what they had heard tell but not seen. Booking after booking from America was cancelled. Florence did not have the great recovery season she had expected.

In this again the young of Florence were neither grateful nor ungrateful. They were attacking not american citizens but the war fever of governments. They were attacking the system which gave such governments such power and made them feel powerless to alter that system. Not a florentine power, but a foreign one, world-controlling, which threatened them in Florence as part of the system and which they knew no other way of reaching.

This is the same old story. This is Florence in its home. No Florentine will ever consent to be told what he must be, still less who he must be; and least of all by foreign dominations. He is himself by his own selection.

The new generation is the future of Florence. May their successors bless them for what they will make of themselves! And of us.

Envoy

Most cities are women.

To be with a woman is to be part of her: which is a reciprocal thing.

One is proud of Edinburgh when one is a part of her. If one is a part of Florence one can also be proud of oneself.

But no man can explain why he is a part of the woman he is with, nor give reasons for loving her.

Booklist

In addition to the usual books of reference I would append:

Indro Montanelli: *Dante e il Suo Secolo* (Milano 1964).

Piero Bargellini: *Vedere e Capire Firenze* (Firenze 1958).

Giuliana Artom Treves: *The Golden Ring* (English edition: London 1956).

Paolo Toschi: *Le Origini del Teatro Italiano* (Torino 1955).

Enrico Barfucci: *Lorenzo de' Medici e la società artistica del suo tempo* (Firenze 1964).

Carlo Segré: *Itinerari di Stranieri in Italia* (Milano 1938).

Luigi Ugolini: *Firenze Viva* (Torino 1962).

Cyril Ray: *The Wines of Italy* (London, etc., 1966).

'Jarro' (G. Piccini): *Il Teatro della Pergola* (Firenze 1912).

Franco Nencini: *Firenze i Giorni del Diluvio* (Firenze 1967, published in English by George Allen & Unwin, 1967: *Florence, the Days of the Flood*).

Firenze Domani (Firenze 1967)

and the illustrated monograph on *Florence* published by the BBC which was finished just before the Flood.

Appendix: The Italian Police System

I have now counted thirteen:

1. *Carabinieri* — Ministry of Defence and Ministry of the Interior.

2. *Corpo Guardia di Pubblica Sicurezza* — Under the Questura (Government, not State).

3. *Polizia Ferroviaria* — Ministry of Transport.

4. *Polizia Postale* — Ministry of Communications.

5. *Guardia di Finanza* — Ministry of Finance. with a specialised branch *Polizia Tributaria* — Deals with bills, receipts, etc.

6. *Polizia Stradale* — Under the State.

7. *Polizia Portuale* — Ministry of Interior, Ministry of Sea Finance and under local Port Captain.

8. *Corpo Forestale dello Stato* — Ministry of Agriculture and Forests.

9. *Guardia Venatoria* — 'Huntsmen.'

10. *Agenti del Dazio* — Local Comune. Tolls on consumer goods entering towns.

11. *Polizia Urbana* — Local Comune.

12. *Polizia Annonaria* — Function unknown except in times of rationing.

13. *Guardie Giurate* — Private. Night patrols against burglars.

All have various specialised sub-sections, for instance the Squadra Politica!

Index